contents

What this book is about: eating for life

Unlike other books on kids' food, this one doesn't preach an evangelical diet, nor assume you have plenty of time to cook interesting meals. It's about feeding your child in the real world – healthily.

Here I've endeavoured to combine my expertise as a nutritionist, my knowledge as a health writer and my experience as a mother. It's one thing to know what children ought to eat, it's another making them eat it. Many a time has my patience been tested as my own children refuse vegetables, reject balanced meals, or pester me in the supermarket for foods they've seen advertised on the TV.

I also know how difficult it can be to say no when children insist on unhealthy snacks because their friends eat them, or when they'd rather nibble on chocolate than an orange. I also know how demanding it is preparing endless healthy meals and snacks and I am well aware of the amount of patience needed to survive family mealtimes.

That's why I wanted to share some of my tips in this book. This second edition of *Healthy Eating for Kids* includes new sections on kids' fitness, feeding active kids, food labels and school meals. I have also added new information from scientific studies on kids' nutrition as well as some new recipes. Most of the recipes now have lovely colour photos to inspire you to make them – hopefully!

One thing is clear: what children eat now has a big impact on their health, fitness and – importantly – what they'll be eating in years to come. Establishing healthy eating habits today will give your children the best start in life.

To make it easier, try following these ten 10 key steps:

1   Teach by example – if they see you enjoying healthy meals, they're more likely to do the same.

2   Keep to the 80/20 rule – if children eat a balanced diet around 80 per cent of the time, then they're free to enjoy other foods they want the other 20 per cent of the time.

3   Be consistent – decide on your ground rules (what is and isn't allowed) and stick to them.

4   Be persistent – children's tastes change and they will eventually learn to like what they're given.

5   Involve them – include your children in menu planning, shopping and cooking as early as possible.

6   Share mealtimes when you can and feed your children the same food you eat yourself.

7   Make children feel valued – that way they'll be more likely to make healthier food and activity choices.

8   Don't ban any food – it will only increase your child's desire for it – and don't use food as a reward.

9   Make meals as attractive, varied and imaginative as you can.

10 Keep treat foods as treats and bring them into the house only on special occasions.

I hope you'll find this book useful and inspirational.

Anita

acknowledgements

Thanks as ever to my husband, Simon, for keeping cool during life's most hectic moments; and to my beautiful daughters, Chloe and Lucy, for giving me the opportunities to put everything in this book into practice – including shopping trips, family mealtime tactics, packing their lunchboxes, devising healthy menus and recipes (that they will eat), cooking with them (and putting up with a very messy kitchen!) – but, best of all, for rewarding me with their enthusiasm for, and love of, healthy food.

I would also like to thank Linda Bird for her editorial expertise, and the wonderful team at A & C Black, especially Charlotte Croft, Rob Foss and Lucy Beevor for making this book possible.

Anita's daughters: Chloe (left) and Lucy (right).

foreword

I was delighted when asked to write the foreword for this second edition. I have recommended the first edition of *Healthy Eating for Kids* to many of the families I worked with at the Carnegie Weight Management Programme, the only residential weight loss programme for children in Europe.

Obesity is a rapidly increasing health threat for children in this country. One in three children in the UK are overweight or obese. This will lead to a significant increase in childhood/adult diabetes, cancer and heart conditions, as well as bullying and discrimination. Of greater concern, though, are the reports that many in this generation of children are unlikely to outlive their parents. It's important for our children and their children that we tackle the obesity problem because if we don't we shall be storing up major health problems. If present trends continue, at least one million children will be obese by 2010.

Children are eating too many snacks, fast foods and ready meals that are high in fat, sugar and salt. They are also spending more time in front of the TV or computer and not taking enough physical activity. Too many children get driven to school and schools have reduced the actual time spent on P.E.

A book about children's nutrition therefore needs to be both comprehensive and inspiring. It requires lots of practical ideas and strategies to help parents overcome the problems of feeding their children healthy foods.

Anita has successfully combined all of these ingredients resulting in a book that is accurate and exciting and written in an easy to follow style. *Healthy Eating for Kids* is written with considerable expertise and I am sure it will go a long way to helping parents feed their children well.

Here, she brings together years of expertise as a nutritionist, as well as a mother who understands the challenge of feeding children. This book is packed with useful facts, clever tips, tasty recipes and inspiring ideas that will transform family meal times and your child's nutrition – for good.

Enjoy!

Professor Paul Gately BA (Hons) MMedSci PhD
Professor in Exercise & Obesity and Founder/Technical Director of the Carnegie International Children's Weight Loss Camp, Leeds Metropolitan University

1 what should children eat?

What children eat affects their health both now and in the future. They need a balanced diet to grow properly, keep healthy and fight off illnesses. A nutritious diet means your children will:

- have plenty of energy
- feel bright and alert
- concentrate better at school
- suffer fewer illnesses
- have clear skin, bright eyes and shiny hair.

Changing children's eating habits not only improves their health but also their behaviour, mood and learning success at school. Primary schools that belong to the government's national healthy schools programme where pupils are better fed and get more exercise, make greater academic progress and outperform others in national tests in reading, maths and science.

Studies at Oxford University show that diet may even help prevent and manage developmental conditions such as ADHD, dyslexia, dyspraxia and autism spectrum disorders as well as mental health conditions such as anxiety and depression.

Studies in the USA (carried out in 2005) have shown that banning school vending machines and providing nutrition education and healthier food options results in better behaviour and academic standards among 5–10 year olds. After one year exclusions had fallen by 80 per cent and school test scores in maths and English had shot up.

The earlier you teach children healthy eating and exercise habits, the better. A healthy diet now means a healthy diet in ten years' time. Children don't 'grow out of' poor eating habits – they continue eating the foods they're used to being given. An overweight teenager has a 70 per cent chance of becoming an overweight adult.

You are their role model!

Kids learn eating and exercise habits from their parents. A 2005 study at Arizona State University, USA, showed that parents who don't monitor their children's diets are more likely to have children who grow up to become overweight or obese.

With two million overweight and 700,000 obese children in the UK, we could be facing a looming epidemic of obesity. The Chief Medical Officer for England, in his 2002 Annual Report, describes childhood obesity as a 'public health time bomb'. Children are more likely to do as you do, so being a good role model will encourage good habits. A 2004 study carried out by University College London found that the more often parents ate fruit and vegetables, the more likely it was their children would have a high intake. Eating a lot of high-fat, salty or sugary foods conditions a child's tastes to those types of food. Unless you make an effort, children will continue to choose bland processed food and reject fresh food such as fruit or vegetables, even though fresh food has stronger flavours. You can't blame them for choosing and eating what they are accustomed to.

It's not always easy to persuade children to make healthy choices but try to stick to the 80/20 rule. This means eating a balanced diet around 80 per cent of the time, while the other 20 per cent of the time children are free to enjoy other foods they want.

What are children eating?

Snacking, grazing and eating on the hoof are the norm for many children as they are moving away from regular mealtimes. According to a 2001 British Medical Association survey, a quarter of British children eat a breakfast of crisps and sweets before they arrive at school in the morning. One in five children aged between 11 and 16 years miss breakfast altogether. The National Diet and Nutrition Survey of British Schoolchildren in 2000 revealed that the most commonly eaten foods among 4–18 year olds are white bread, crisps, biscuits, potatoes and chocolate bars. Fewer than half the children ate green leafy vegetables. This survey, the largest of its kind, looked at the diets of 1701 children over seven days and found that:

- Children are eating a mere two portions of fruit and vegetables per day (five portions daily are recommended).

- One in five children eat no fruit at all.

- More than 90 per cent of children are eating too much saturated fat.

- Most children eat twice the maximum recommended amount of salt.

- Half of all girls aged 11–18 years eat diets grossly deficient in iron and magnesium.

- Children are eating more than the maximum recommended amount of sugar.

It's when these poor eating habits are coupled with inactivity – watching television, playing computer games and getting around by car all the time – that the trouble really begins. Too many calories and too little exercise will cause an unhealthy increase in body fat.

Why should you change what children eat?

If children eat a healthy diet now, and participate in physical activity from an early age, they are more likely to remain healthy and active during adulthood. Children who are used to eating vegetables or walking to school every day (even when it rains) will continue to eat healthy food and see activity as an integral part of their life. Equally, those who graze on a diet of fast food and salty snacks and spend hours glued to the television are setting themselves up for a lifetime of poor eating habits and inactivity.

It's also important to realise that the seeds of certain illnesses, such as coronary heart disease and diabetes, are sown during childhood. Overweight children as young as 10 years old are showing signs of artery damage and suffering from high blood pressure. The good news is that changing children's diets and encouraging them to be more active can prevent health problems in the future.

What is a balanced diet?

Eating a balanced diet is all about eating a wide variety of foods. Your children's diet should provide them with all the vital nutrients needed to keep them fit and well. A healthy diet consists of a balance of protein, carbohydrate, fat, vitamins and minerals.

The easiest way to plan your children's diet is by using the Children's Food Guide Pyramid, shown on page 16. It is loosely based on the nutritional recommendations of the 2005 US Department of Agriculture's Food Guidance System for kids (*see* www.mypyramid.gov). It recommends a diet rich in fruit and vegetables, and including whole grains and healthy fats. It discourages saturated fats, trans fats and refined carbohydrates and tells you how many portions of each food group children should aim to have each day. The foods at the bottom of the pyramid should make up the largest proportion of their diet, while the foods at the top of the pyramid should be eaten in smaller amounts.

Make sure you:

■ include foods from each food group in the pyramid every day

■ choose a variety of foods from each group

■ provide the recommended number of portions from each food group each day

■ check the portion sizes suggested on the next page.

APPROXIMATE DAILY NUTRITIONAL NEEDS OF CHILDREN				
FOOD GROUP	**NUMBER OF PORTIONS EACH DAY**	**FOOD**	**PORTION SIZE (5–8 YEARS)**	**PORTION SIZE (9–12 YEARS)**
Vegetables	3		*The amount a child can hold in their hand*	
		Broccoli, cauliflower	1–2 spears/florets	2–3 spears/florets
		Carrots	1 small carrot	1 carrot
		Peas	2 tablespoons	3 tablespoons
		Other vegetables	2 tablespoons	3 tablespoons
		Tomatoes	3 cherry tomatoes	5 cherry tomatoes
Fruit	2		*The amount a child can hold in their hand*	
		Apple, pear, peach, banana	1 small fruit	1 medium fruit
		Plum, kiwi fruit, satsuma	1 fruit	1–2 fruit
		Strawberries	6	8–10
		Grapes	8–12	12–16
		Tinned fruit	2 tablespoons	3 tablespoons
		Fruit juice	1 small glass	1 medium glass
Grains and potatoes	4–6		*The size of a child's fist*	
		Bread	1 small slice	1 slice
		Rolls/muffins	½ roll	1 roll
		Pasta or rice	3 tablespoons	4 tablespoons
		Breakfast cereal	3 tablespoons	4 tablespoons
		Potatoes, sweet potatoes, yams	1 fist-sized	1 fist-sized
Calcium-rich foods	2	Milk (dairy or calcium-fortified soya milk)	1 small cup	1 medium cup
		Cheese	Size of 4 dice	Size of 4 dice
		Tofu	Size of 4 dice	Size of 4 dice
		Tinned sardines	1 tablespoon	1–2 tablespoons
		Yoghurt/fromage frais	1 pot	1 pot
Protein-rich foods	2		*The size of a child's palm*	
		Lean meat	1 slice (40 g)	1–2 slices (40–80 g)
		Poultry	2 thin slices/1 small breast	2 medium slices/1 breast
		Fish	Half a fillet	1 fillet
		Egg	1	1–2
		Lentils/beans	2 tablespoons	3 tablespoons
		Tofu/soya burger or sausage	1 small	1 medium
Healthy fats and oils	1	Nuts and seeds	1 tablespoon	1 heaped tablespoon
		Seed oils, nut oils	2 teaspoons	1 tablespoon
		Oily fish*	60 g (2 oz)	85 g (3 oz)

*Oily fish is very rich in essential fats so just 1 portion a week would more than cover a child's daily needs

How many portions a day?

Try to include the suggested number of portions of each food group each day. Remember, these are guidelines and on some days children may need more or less of a certain food group.

Grains and potatoes

4–6 portions daily

   Bread, pasta, rice, noodles, breakfast cereals, porridge oats, crackers, potatoes, sweet potatoes, parsnips and yams.

   Benefits: Rich energy sources, providing carbohydrates, B vitamins, iron and other minerals. Try to make at least half of your child's portions wholegrain rather than 'white', i.e. wholemeal bread, wholegrain breakfast cereals and wholewheat pasta. These foods are an important source of fibre, which helps to keep the digestive system healthy and prevent constipation.

   The glycaemic index (GI) is a measure of how the body reacts to foods containing carbohydrate. Sugary foods and refined ('white') starchy foods have a high GI, which means they raise blood sugar levels rapidly. If children eat lots of high GI foods they may develop problems with blood sugar control and you'll certainly notice a change in their energy levels and mood. Some children are particularly sensitive to sugar and other high GI foods, which means their blood sugar level rises too quickly when they eat something sugary. This makes the pancreas pump out extra insulin, which, in turn, brings blood sugar levels down again too quickly. This rapid fall can make children feel tired, grumpy and irritable a lot of the time. They will also be prone to poor concentration, 'foggy brain' and, in older children, underachievement and delinquent behaviour.

   Prevent blood sugar peaks and troughs by focusing on low GI eating through the day. Base meals on low GI foods (e.g. porridge or pasta dishes) and encourage low GI snacks, such as fresh fruit, nuts and seeds. High GI foods (e.g. white bread) are fine in small quantities or, better still, combined with a low GI food (e.g. baked beans) or a protein-rich food (e.g. tuna or cheese). Low GI meals and snacks will help keep children full of energy during the day. They also tend to make children feel satisfied for longer and less inclined to snack.

LOW GI FOODS	MEDIUM GI FOODS	HIGH GI FOODS
Pasta	Brown and basmati rice	White bread and rolls, French bread and bagels
Baked beans (and other types of beans and lentils)	Pizza	Most breakfast cereals, e.g. cornflakes, rice crispies, coco pops
Milk	Chapatti	White rice
Peas	Pitta bread	Most wholemeal bread
Most vegetables, e.g. cucumber, broccoli	Boiled potatoes	Mashed and baked potatoes
Most fresh fruit, e.g. apples, pears, bananas, grapes, kiwi fruit	Carrots	Doughnuts
	Tinned fruit	Chips
Dried apricots	Ice cream	Jam and sugar
Nuts	Raisins	Soft drinks
Porridge and muesli	Muesli bars	Sweets
Multigrain bread (e.g. Granary)	Digestive biscuits	Most biscuits

Ten low GI meals

1 Jacket potato with baked beans
2 Fish pie
3 Pasta with tomato sauce and cheese
4 Pitta bread filled with chicken (or cheese) and cucumber
5 Porridge with raisins
6 Cheese and tomato pizza with extra veggies
7 Pasta with sweetcorn and tuna
8 Macaroni cheese
9 Chicken and vegetable curry with basmati rice
10 Tomato or lentil soup with granary bread

Ten low GI snacks

1 Cheese (or egg) on toast
2 Rice cakes or crackers with peanut butter
3 Carrot batons with a cheesy dip or hummus
4 Apple or banana
5 Fruit cake
6 Dried apricots
7 Pancakes
8 Yoghurt
9 Milkshake or flavoured milk
10 Nuts and raisins

Fruit and vegetables
Five portions daily

All types of fruit, vegetables and salad. Fruit juice and smoothies can count as one portion towards the five-a-day target.

Benefits: Rich sources of many vitamins and minerals and other plant nutrients (phytonutrients) that are important for health and fighting off illnesses. Eating more fruit and veg means taking in more vitamins, such as vitamin C for a strong immune system, and minerals, such as magnesium for healthy bones. Try to include as many different types of fruit and vegetables as possible and mix colours for maximum nutritional benefits.

Calcium-rich foods
Two portions daily

Milk, soya milk (fortified with calcium), cheese, yoghurt, fromage frais, tofu, tinned fish with edible bones (e.g. sardines), dark green leafy vegetables.

Benefits: Rich sources of calcium, which is important for building healthy bones and teeth. These foods also supply protein and B vitamins. If your children don't like dairy foods, make sure you offer alternative calcium sources (see above).

Protein-rich foods
Two portions daily

Lean meat, chicken, turkey, fish, eggs, beans, lentils, nuts, and soya and quorn products.

Benefits: These foods are important sources of protein, which is needed for growth, repair and development, as well as good amounts of B vitamins, iron and zinc.

Children need about 1 g per kg of body weight (adults need 0.75 g/kg). For example, a child who weighs 40 kg should eat about 40 g of protein daily. The Recommended Daily Amounts for protein are shown in the box opposite. They can meet their protein needs by including two portions of protein-rich food in their daily diet as well as grains and dairy foods, which also supply smaller amounts of protein.

Vegetarian children need to eat a wide variety of plant proteins: beans, lentils, grains, nuts, seeds, soya and quorn.

tip *Provide as much variety as possible. Aim for a mix of colours: orange/yellow, red, green, purple, white.*

WHAT ABOUT VEGETARIANS?

Vegetarians may substitute extra dairy food for one of the portions in the protein-rich group, as dairy foods are also rich in protein. For example, aim for three portions of dairy foods plus one portion of protein-rich foods. However, don't eliminate this group entirely as these foods supply valuable vitamins and minerals not present in dairy foods.

tip *Even if your family isn't vegetarian, try to introduce some vegetable protein foods (beans, lentils and soya) into your children's diet. These foods provide a unique type of fibre that's beneficial for the digestive system, as well as important plant nutrients.*

DAILY PROTEIN REQUIREMENTS OF CHILDREN		
AGE GROUP	BOYS	GIRLS
4–6 years	19.7 g	19.7 g
7–10 years	28.3 g	28.3 g
11–14 years	42.1 g	41.2 g
15–18 years	55.2 g	45.0 g

Source: Dept of Health Dietary Reference Values for food energy and nutrients for the United Kingdom (1991) London: HMSO

tip *Use lean cuts of meat and limit sausages, burgers and nuggets to no more than two portions a week because they contain a lot of saturated fat and salt.*

Healthy fats and oils
At least one portion daily

Nuts (walnuts, cashews, almonds, pecans, Brazils, pine nuts), seeds (sesame, pumpkin, sunflower), seed and nut oils (e.g. olive, rapeseed, sunflower) and oily fish (e.g. sardines, mackerel, pilchards).

Benefits: Excellent sources of 'good' fats: the omega-3 and omega-6 fats, and monounsaturated fats, essential for health.

Q&A

Question: Can Omega 3 fats improve learning behaviour?

Answer: Increasing omega-3 intake (with supplements) may improve behaviour and learning in *some* children. All of the trials to date have involved children with specific behavioural and learning difficulties such as ADHD, dyslexia or dyspraxia. A 2006 trial of 117 children aged 5–12 years in a Durham primary school carried out by Oxford University researchers (the largest so far) showed some remarkable improvements in both behaviour and learning. Children who took omega-3 supplements for three months improved their reading ability more than three times the normal rate and more than twice the rate in spelling, over three months of treatment. There were also significant improvements in their ADHD symptoms.

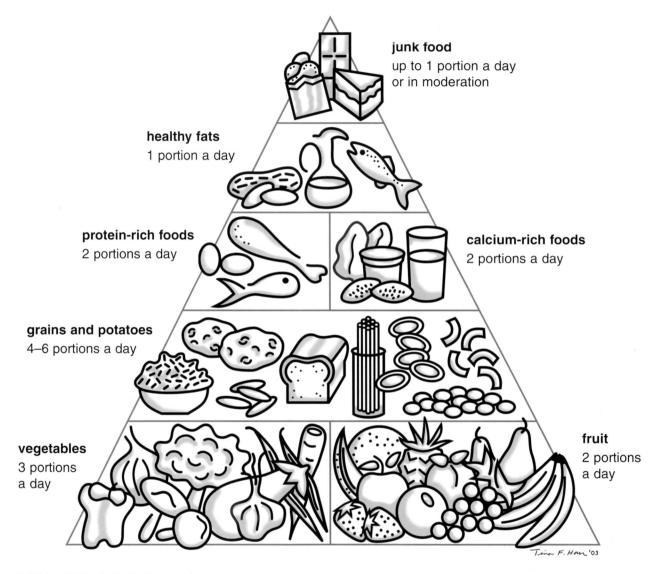

junk food
up to 1 portion a day
or in moderation

healthy fats
1 portion a day

protein-rich foods
2 portions a day

calcium-rich foods
2 portions a day

grains and potatoes
4–6 portions a day

vegetables
3 portions
a day

fruit
2 portions
a day

Children's Food Guide Pyramid

FOODS THAT PROVIDE OMEGA-3 FATS

- ▪ Oily fish (sardines, mackerel, salmon, herring, pilchards, trout, fresh tuna) and seafood

- ▪ Omega-3 eggs

- ▪ Omega-3 fortified milk, margarine, bread and fruit juice

- ▪ Wild game and organic meat

- ▪ Walnuts and smaller amounts in other nuts

- ▪ Dark green leafy vegetables

- ▪ Sweet potatoes

- ▪ Pumpkin seeds and pumpkinseed oil

- ▪ Flaxseed and flaxseed oil

- ▪ Rapeseed oil and soya oil

WHY CHILDREN NEED OMEGA-3 FATS

- ▪ Normal brain development

- ▪ Normal eyesight

- ▪ Help nervous system work

- ▪ Strengthen immune system

- ▪ Keep joints supple

- ▪ Healthy heart and circulation

- ▪ Growing evidence suggests that a lack of omega-3 fats may contribute to developmental conditions of learning and behaviour, such as dyslexia, dyspraxia and ADHD (which affects around 1 in 20 children)

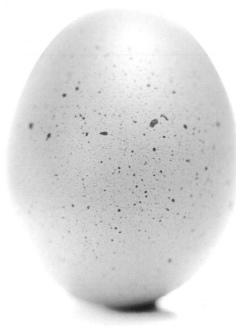

Q&A

Question: Should I give my children omega-3 supplements?

Answer: Omega-3 supplements may benefit children with learning difficulties. In particular, they may reduce problems such as low attention, poor concentration, visual symptoms, mood swings, anxiety, sleep problems and eczema. However, there is no proof that supplements increase academic performance or IQ in other children.

Fatty and sugary foods

Try to limit these foods to one portion daily

Biscuits, cakes, sweets, confectionery, soft drinks, chocolate, crisps and other savoury snacks.

These foods are high in saturated fat, added sugar and/or salt. They provide lots of calories but few, if any, essential nutrients.

FISH OIL

Fish oil contains two major omega-3 fatty acids: eicosapentanoic acid (EPA) and docosahexanoic acid (DHA). DHA is needed in early life for the growing brain. EPA is needed for normal brain function and can reduce problems associated with ADHD, dyslexia and dyspraxia.

NUT ALLERGIES

Nuts can cause serious allergies in a small proportion of children, and peanuts seem to cause the worst reaction. The exact cause is not known but children with nut allergies often have other allergies and other allergy-related conditions such as asthma, hay fever and eczema. A family history of allergy also increases the risk of a child developing a nut allergy. Early signs may include a mild tingling in the mouth or more obvious swelling in the mouth, difficulty in breathing and swallowing, culminating, occasionally, in anaphylactic shock, which can kill if not dealt with quickly.

It is recommended that young children under three years old with a family history of allergy should not be given peanuts in any form. Children with no allergy history can be given peanuts and other nut products after the age of one. Whole nuts should not be given to children under five years old because of the risk of choking, but they can be used finely ground or as peanut butter.

Salt and children's health

We should avoid eating too much salt, whatever our age. This is because salt contains sodium and having too much sodium can cause raised blood pressure, which increases the risk of heart disease and stroke.

It's important to keep an eye on how much salt your child is consuming. Children under seven years old should have no more than 3 g of salt a day. Those between seven and ten years should have no more than 5 g daily and those aged 11+ years no more than 6 g daily. Children are particularly vulnerable to the effects of salt. Despite requiring less salt than adults, the average child in the UK consumes as much as 10–12 g per day.

Lots of processed foods are high in salt, including many products aimed at children. So you might not realise how much salt your child is eating. Processed foods include everything from breakfast cereals and biscuits to soups and tinned spaghetti. A small can of pasta shapes and mini sausages in tomato sauce contains 2.5 g of salt, almost the entire guideline daily maximum for six-year-old children. A cheeseburger with a small portion of fries contains 3.3 g salt, which is 10 per cent more than the daily maximum intake. Cutting their salt intake will benefit their health now and in the future. A 2006 study at St George's Medical School, London, found that reducing children's salt intake significantly reduces children's blood pressure.

How to reduce children's salt intake

- Limit tinned foods, such as pasta shapes in tomato sauce and baked beans. Buy reduced salt versions (although they are still quite high in salt and may also contain artificial sweeteners) or remove some of the sauce.

- Cut down on burgers, sausages and chicken nuggets – one portion contains around half of their daily salt maximum.

- Limit the number of salty snacks such as crisps and biscuits. Instead, give them low-salt snacks such as dried fruit, raw vegetable sticks, grapes and satsumas.

- Check labels on food to see how much salt is listed on the packaging. Try to choose foods that contain less than 0.25 g salt per 100 g.

- Cut down on ready-made sauces – one portion of pasta sauce contains around a third of a child's daily maximum.

AGE	GUIDELINE DAILY AMOUNT (GDA)
4–6 years	3 g
7–10 years	5 g
11+ years	6 g

- Look for bread with lower levels of salt or those made with salt replacer. Two slices of ordinary bread contain around 1 g of salt.

- Make your own soup – ready-made tinned or fresh soup contains up to 2.5 g of salt per portion.

- Make sure they have plenty of fruit and vegetables. They are rich in the mineral potassium, which helps balance out some of the harmful effects of salt.

SALT CONTENTS OF VARIOUS FOODS (PER TYPICAL CHILD'S PORTION)	
Chicken nuggets	1.8 g
Pizza	1.3 g
Tin of beans	2.5 g
Doughnut	1.2 g
Hamburger	2.0 g
Milkshake	0.5 g
Sugar-coated cereal	1.5 g
Tin of spaghetti	2.3 g
2 fish fingers	1.3 g
Pasta sauce	1.0 g
Crisps	0.6 g
Shepherd's pie ready meal	1.9 g

CHECK THE LABEL

To see if a product is high in salt, according to the Food Standards Agency recommendations, compare the amount per 100 g with the following guidelines (or check the traffic light label found on certain products).

SALT:
More than 1.25 g is high
Less than 0.25 g is low

SODIUM:
More than 0.5 g is high
Less than 0.1 g is low

1 g of sodium is equivalent to 2.5 g of salt.

Sugar

Foods and drinks containing sugar shouldn't be eaten too often as they can contribute to tooth decay. They also tend to be high in calories and fat, and low in valuable nutrients. As a result, a high-sugar diet is often linked with obesity.

The World Health Organisation recommends that adults and children should get no more than 10 per cent of daily calories from sugar. But, on average, British children get around 17 per cent of their daily energy needs from sugar – considerably higher than the recommended maximum. Ideally, children aged 4–6 years should eat no more than 40 g (2½ tablespoons) a day, 7–10 years and 11–14 years no more than 50 g (3½ tablespoons).

Sugar doesn't just come from obvious foods such as soft drinks, biscuits, cakes, sweets, chocolate and desserts. Yoghurt, ready meals, breakfast cereals, sauces and baked beans contain high levels of added sugar (see the sugar guide on page 23).

CHECK THE LABEL

To see if a product is high in sugar according to the Food Standards Agency recommendations, compare the amount per 100 g with the following guidelines (or check the traffic light label found on certain products).

More than 10 g is high
Less than 2 g is low

Caution! No added sugar doesn't mean the food is low in sugar – it may contain other ingredients such as fruit juice with a high natural sugar content.

HIDDEN SUGAR

Look out for sucrose, glucose syrup, dextrose, fruit syrup and glucose on food labels – they all mean sugar. The main problem with sugar is that it damages children's teeth.

How to cut down on sugar

- Don't ban sweets and chocolate completely – limit them to certain clearly defined occasions. For example, allow one 'treat' every Saturday after supper. If your children are given sweets on other days, they can save them for Saturday.

- Keep any food and drink containing sugar mainly to mealtimes to reduce the risk of tooth decay.

- Check the labels for hidden sugars (e.g. glucose syrup, dextrose) and try to choose foods that contain less than 2 g of sugar per 100 g.

- Limit soft drinks, sweets, biscuits, cakes and puddings. Even artificially sweetened varieties encourage a liking for sugar.

- Don't add unnecessary sugar to food.

- Use more unprocessed foods that are naturally sweet (e.g. fresh and dried fruit) – they contain more vitamins and fibre.

- Give plain water to drink. If your children aren't keen on it, give fruit juice diluted with water – you can gradually add less juice and more water.

Q&A

Question: Is it better to give children sugar-free products that contain artificial sweeteners instead of sugar?

Answer: Artificial sweeteners, such as aspartame acesulphane K and saccharin, may not decay children's teeth but they still encourage intensely sweet tastes. The government considers them safe – although they're not allowed in baby foods – but some scientists argue that high intakes may be linked with migraines and brain tumours. In moderation, there's probably little danger to children's health. But why not get sweetness from fresh or dried fruit or just have small amounts of sweet foods, such as good chocolate, which have no artificial sweeteners?

AGE	GUIDELINE DAILY AMOUNT (GDA) OF SUGAR
4–6 years	40 g (2½ tablespoons)
7–10 years	50 g (3 tablespoons)
11–14 years	50 g (3½ tablespoons)
15–18 years	60 g (4 tablespoons)

Source: Institute of Grocery Distribution, GDA Technical Working Group, 2005

Sugar guide	
Can of cola	7 teaspoons
Glass of fruit drink or squash	4 teaspoons
Chocolate bar	8 teaspoons
2 biscuits	2 teaspoons
1 tablespoon tomato ketchup	1 teaspoon
Small can of baked beans/ pasta shapes	2 teaspoons
2 scoops ice cream	4½ teaspoons
1 pot of fruit yoghurt	3 teaspoons
Small bowl of sugar-coated cereal	3 teaspoons
Small bowl of chocolate cereal	3 teaspoons
1 breakfast cereal bar	2 teaspoons
1 fruit snack roll	3 teaspoons

Looking after children's teeth

Eating lots of sugary foods increases the chance of tooth decay, especially if children eat them frequently throughout the day. Fruit, fruit juice, fruit drinks and squash can also cause enamel erosion – literally dissolving the tooth away – because they contain fruit acids. Help to prevent tooth decay and erosion by:

■ Encouraging children to brush their teeth with a little fluoride toothpaste twice a day (after breakfast and before bed) and shortly after eating sugary foods.

■ Milk is a far 'safer' drink for teeth. Fruit juice diluted at least one part juice to one part water is better than squash, fruit drinks and fizzy drinks.

■ Discouraging sugary or sticky foods between meals. These leave residues on the teeth, increasing the risk of decay. Note: dried fruit is as potentially harmful to teeth as sweets!

■ If sugary foods or drinks are eaten, then it is better to finish them quickly rather than sucking a packet of sweets or sipping a drink.

■ Encouraging the drinking of acidic drinks with a straw. This reduces the contact of the drink with the teeth. Sugar-free drinks aren't necessarily better for children's teeth as they are quite acidic and can cause dental erosion.

■ Eating a small piece of cheese at the end of a meal or after a sugary or acidic snack helps counteract the harmful effects of sugar. Cheese is alkaline and rich in calcium, and neutralises the fruit acids.

RASPBERRY FOOL

This dessert contains no added sugar. The sweetness is provided by a little honey and the natural sugars in the raspberries. It is also packed with vitamin C. You can substitute other seasonal fruits such as strawberries, blackberries or, in the winter, mango or stewed apple.

MAKES 4 SERVINGS

- *225 g (8 oz) raspberries*
- *225 g (8 oz) low-fat plain fromage frais*
- *1 tbsp (15 ml) clear honey*

1 *Mash the raspberries lightly with a fork.*
2 *Mix with the fromage frais and honey. Spoon into 4 bowls.*

Q&A

Question: What are the healthiest drinks to give children?

Answer: The best drinks to give children are water, milk, and flavoured milk and milkshakes with less than 5 per cent added sugar (up to 10 per cent added sugar in milk does not harm teeth).

Fruit juice is also a healthy drink – it contains valuable vitamins and minerals and can count as one portion towards the five-a-day target – but should be diluted at least one to one with water. Juice contains natural sugars that can damage teeth, especially if your children sip it from a bottle or drink it frequently. Try to keep fruit juice to mealtimes. This is better for teeth than drinking it between meals.

Smoothies contain the whole fruit so they are a good way of boosting vitamin, mineral and fibre intakes. They count as one of a child's five fruit and veg portions a day. Check the label to make sure it contains no added sugar or additives.

Squash, juice drinks, fizzy drinks and some brands of milkshake contain high levels of added sugar, which is also bad for teeth. Diluting squash well will make it less sugary, but again try to keep it to mealtimes.

All fizzy drinks, including diet varieties, contain very few nutrients. They can also be very filling, so they could reduce your children's appetite for food that contains the nutrients they need.

SNACKS AND DRINKS THAT ARE SAFER FOR TEETH	
SNACKS	**DRINKS**
Fresh fruit	Water
Yoghurt (preferably unsweetened)	Milk
Cheese (with crackers or bread)	Diluted fruit juice
Toast, plain or with Marmite,	(1 or 2 parts water to
peanut butter or cheese	1 part juice)
Nuts	
Vegetable sticks with dips	
Savoury sandwiches	

How to get children to drink more water

■ If your children are used to sweet drinks, wean them off gradually by diluting squash with extra water or offering fruit juice mixed with an equal amount of water. This will help retrain their palates to accept less sweetness.

■ Add slices of lemon or lime to water or frozen cubes of fruit juice to water.

■ Make drinking more fun with a novelty water bottle.

■ Set a healthy example: drink water yourself.

■ Try keeping a chart to make your children aware of how much they drink.

■ Have a jug of water on the table at mealtimes.

SUGAR IN FRUIT

Fruit is a natural source of sugar, but fruit also contains fibre and vitamins that balance out the sugar.

HOW TO GET CHILDREN TO EAT A HEALTHIER DIET

■ Explain the benefits of eating more healthily. This should be in terms that your children can understand and directly relate to, e.g. having more energy to play football; feeling more refreshed in the morning.

■ Put children in control of some of their food choices, e.g. allow them to choose which vegetables to eat; let them suggest a new meal.

■ Make some realistic goals (e.g. to eat two pieces of fruit a day; to try a new vegetable; to replace crisps with an apple or a handful of nuts).

■ Set up a reward system, e.g. award a star or sticker for each healthy eating behaviour. When, for example, 10 stars have been earned, choose a reward (preferably non-food, such as a new toy or a special trip) that has been agreed upon in advance.

■ Increase the range of foods in your family's repertoire – try new recipes and offer new snacks (see recipes on pages 149–154).

■ Set a good example yourself — don't show reservation in trying new foods.

■ Praise children for trying a new food. Even if they don't like it, encourage them to explain why. Try the motto: 'taste before you judge' – it always works with my children who end up eating the lot!

■ If a new food or dish is rejected initially, leave it for a while then re-introduce it a week or so later. Children will eventually like healthy foods if they are continually exposed to them.

Summary

■ If children learn to enjoy a balanced diet now, they'll continue to eat well and stay healthy as they get older.

■ Keep to the 80/20 rule – if children eat a balanced diet around 80 per cent of the time, they're free to enjoy other foods they want the other 20 per cent of the time.

- Each day children should aim to have five portions of fruit and vegetables, four to six portions of grains and potatoes, two portions of protein-rich foods, two portions of calcium-rich foods and one portion of healthy fats.

- Keep an eye on how much salt your child is having – limit to 3–6 g daily (depending on age).

- Limit food and drinks containing sugar to 40–50 g daily (depending on age). They can contribute to tooth decay and obesity and displace other nutrients in the diet.

- Water, milk or diluted fruit juice are healthier options for teeth.

BANANA MILKSHAKE

This simple, nutritious shake includes no added sugar and is much better for teeth than sugary drinks.

MAKES 2 SERVINGS

- *250 ml (8 fl oz) milk (full-fat or semi-skimmed)*
- *2 ripe bananas, sliced*
- *Few ice cubes, crushed*

1 *Put the milk, crushed ice and banana in a blender. Blend until smooth, thick and bubbly.*

2   going green

How to get kids to eat fruit and vegetables

Getting children to eat the five portions of fruit and vegetables a day recommended by the World Health Organisation and the UK's Food Standards Agency can be a struggle. On average, children in the UK only eat two portions of fruit and veg a day – way short of the recommended amount!

This means that many are missing out on important nutrients. As well as being a great source of fibre, fruit and vegetables are rich in vitamins (especially disease-fighting vitamins A and C), minerals and other important plant nutrients, which help keep children healthy and boost their immunity.

What's a portion?

A child portion is roughly the amount they can hold in their hand – their portion grows as they do! This could be:

Fruit

- 1 small apple, pear, banana or peach
- About 12 grapes
- 1 satsuma, kiwi fruit or plum
- About 6–7 strawberries
- A glass of pure fruit juice
- 2–3 tablespoons tinned fruit
- One tablespoon of raisins, sultanas, dried apricots or dried mango

Vegetable

- 2 tablespoons of peas, cabbage or sweetcorn
- 2 broccoli spears
- 1 cooked carrot or 7–8 carrot sticks
- 3–5 cherry tomatoes
- 7–8 cucumber slices

5-a-day can be achieved by:

Menu 1

1 A glass of orange juice with breakfast

2 An apple as a snack

3 Pizza topped with extra vegetables for lunch

4 A portion of carrots at teatime

5 Fruit mixed with yoghurt for pudding

Menu 2

1 Breakfast cereal topped with banana slices

2 Grapes or banana as a snack

3 Vegetable soup for lunch

4 Carrot, pepper and cucumber sticks or cherry tomatoes at teatime

5 Apple crumble for pudding

Why 5 a day?

- Children will be less likely to get minor infections such as colds and flu if they eat plenty of fruit and veg – particularly those rich in vitamin C, such as oranges, kiwi fruit, red peppers, strawberries and raspberries.

- Five daily portions of fruit and veg help protect against many cancers in later life.

- A high level of fruit and veg in the diet cuts the risk of heart disease and stroke during adulthood.

tip **Try adding vegetables to sauces, soups and pies.** *Vegetables such as chopped carrots, mushrooms and peppers can be added to Bolognese sauce, vegetable soup, lasagne, hot pots, stews, bakes and pies. The tomato in pasta sauce counts as a portion, but try adding a cupful of chopped broccoli, peppers, courgettes or mushrooms.*

CARROT SOUP

This soup is inexpensive and simple to make, and packed with the antioxidant beta-carotene which the body converts into vitamin A and which helps fight disease.

MAKES 4 SERVINGS

- 2 tbsp (30 ml) olive oil
- 1 onion, chopped
- 1 clove of garlic, crushed
- 675 g (1½ lb) carrots, sliced
- 900 ml (1½ pints) vegetable stock*
- Salt and freshly ground black pepper
- 1–2 tablespoons fresh coriander, chopped (optional)

*Alternatively, use 3 tsp (15 ml) Swiss vegetable bouillon or 1½ vegetable stock cubes in 900 ml (1½ pints) water

1 Sauté the onion and garlic in the olive oil for 5 minutes in a large saucepan.
2 Add the carrots and continue cooking for a further 2 minutes.
3 Add the stock and bring to the boil, then reduce the heat and simmer for 15 minutes or until the carrots are tender.
4 Season with the salt and pepper and add the fresh coriander.
5 Liquidise using a hand blender or food processor.

Five ways to eat 5

1 Most children eat three meals and two snacks a day. If they have one portion of fruit or vegetables at each eating occasion, they've hit 5-a-day!

2 Use the Rainbow Rule: every day try to get your child to eat five different colours of fruit or vegetables.

3 Set a good example yourself. Children are more likely to eat fruit and vegetables if they see you enjoying these foods daily and if there's a plentiful supply in the house.

GETTING 5 A DAY

Ideally, aim for two portions of fruit and three portions of vegetables. Variety is key. Mix colours – green, orange, red, yellow, purple – as each colour provides different health benefits.

4 Use a star reward chart to meet their 5-a-day target, giving one star for each daily portion of fruit and veg.

5 Get children involved with the shopping – let them choose a new variety of fruit and vegetable (and then, hopefully, eat it!).

How to make vegetables fun for kids

Do your children struggle to eat their vegetables or refuse to eat anything 'green'? If vegetables aren't included as part of a meal, they'll be missing out on a concentrated source of vitamins and minerals and almost certainly fill up with more pudding, or ask for snacks later on when they get hungry.

Grow your own vegetables

Children will enjoy helping to grow vegetables. Help them plant and harvest their own vegetable garden. Almost any patch of garden soil will do or use a large tray or pot filled with compost. The easiest to grow are potatoes, runner beans, tomatoes, spinach and courgettes. Think of it as a valuable educational experience as children will learn exactly where vegetables come from (not the supermarket!).

Get them in the kitchen

Let your children help wash, peel and cut vegetables. When they feel involved with meal planning and preparation, they're more likely to try new vegetables.

Don't force it

Won't eat spinach or sprouts? Don't fret if your children won't eat a wide range of vegetables. They can get the key nutrients – vitamin C and beta-carotene – from strawberries and carrots. As their tastes develop, they will start to like other vegetables.

Add vegetables to pizzas

Let children decorate their own pizzas with a selection of peppers, sweetcorn, courgettes, mushrooms, tomatoes and pineapple. Or mix finely chopped or pureed vegetables into the tomato sauce before topping the pizza base.

Q&A

Question: *The only vegetable my child seems to want is potatoes – in the form of chips. How can I vary his diet?*

Answer: Unfortunately, potatoes don't count towards the 5-a-day target for fruit and veg – they contain fewer vitamins so are regarded as carbohydrate foods.

Instead of always using potatoes, how about making oven chips from other root vegetables? Cut sweet potatoes, carrots, parsnips, swede, butternut squash or pumpkin into wedges, toss in a little olive or rapeseed oil and pop in the oven at 200°C (400°F or Gas mark 6) for 25–30 minutes.

Hide 'em

You can get children to try a new vegetable if you mix it with a food they already like, such as mashed potato (try adding swede, parsnip, cabbage or spinach), soup, curry or macaroni cheese.

Let them choose

Children like to decide on their own portions so put out dishes and big spoons and let them serve themselves. They're more likely to eat the portion they've chosen than one you've served them!

Start small

If you do serve food straight on to your children's plate, put out tiny portions of two or three vegetables. Large portions can look overwhelming and may not get eaten at all. Children are more likely to eat small portions of two or three different vegetables than one large portion.

Eat 'em raw

Carrot and cucumber sticks, pepper strips, baby sweetcorn and cherry tomatoes make tasty lunchbox foods or teatime nibbles. Serve with hummus, salsa or a cheesy dip. Younger children who refuse most vegetables will often eat 'finger' vegetables.

Try frozen

If you don't always have time to chop vegetables, use pre-prepared or frozen varieties instead. Many frozen vegetables such as peas are just as nutritious as fresh versions as they're frozen within hours of picking.

Q&A

Question: *My children say vegetables are boring and always moan at the sight of them on their plate.*

Answer: Jazz up plain vegetables with a little grated cheese or tomato ketchup. Or combine with a home-made or ready-bought sauce. Broccoli, cauliflower and Brussels sprouts go well with cheese sauce; beans, peas and sweetcorn can be stirred into pasta sauce. Slather salad with a low fat dressing or creamy dip. Forget meat and two veg. All-in-one dishes transform vegetables into meals in their own right: think vegetable curry, vegetable hot pot and vegetable chilli.

Make them attractive

For younger children, try to make vegetables more fun – arrange broccoli and cauliflower as trees on a base of mashed potato; make faces (e.g. use carrots for eyes, baby sweetcorn for a nose, red peppers for the mouth, broccoli for hair, or whatever else your child likes!).

Think tomatoes

Tomato-based pasta sauce as well as tomato soup, tinned tomatoes and passata (pureed tomatoes) count as one portion. Tomatoes are a great source of antioxidants, especially lycopene, which help protect against heart disease and cancer. Add extra vegetables – frozen peas, sweetcorn, mushrooms, or tinned red kidney beans.

KEEP THE VITAMINS IN!

- Buy locally grown produce if you can, ideally from farm shops and local markets. This means the vitamins are less likely to be lost between being picked and being served!

- Buy British if you have a choice – imported produce is usually harvested under-ripe (before it has developed its full vitamin quota) and will have lost much of its nutritional value during its journey to your supermarket.

- Buy fresh-looking, unblemished, undamaged fruit and vegetables.

- Prepare fruit and vegetables just before you make them into a salad or cook them. From the moment they are chopped they start to lose nutrients.

- Fruit and vegetables should be eaten unpeeled wherever possible – many vitamins and minerals are concentrated just beneath the skin.

- Use frozen food if fresh is not available – it's nutritionally similar.

- Cut into large pieces rather than small; vitamins are lost from cut surfaces.

- Steam or boil vegetables in the minimum amount of water to preserve the vitamins.

- When boiling vegetables, add to fast-boiling water and cook as briefly as possible until they're tender-crisp, not soft and mushy.

- Save the cooking water for soups, stocks and sauces.

- Don't re-heat leftover cooked vegetables – they'll have lost most of their nutritional value.

How to make fruit fun

Grow them

If you have the space, try planting an apple, pear or plum tree – children will enjoy the experience of observing the yearly cycle of a fruit tree. Strawberries can be grown in tubs and produce lots of fruit.

Make snacks healthy

Establish nutritious snack habits; make fresh fruit the norm for at least one snack a day. Apple slices, grapes and peeled satsumas are all good choices.

Start early

Get them to have one fruit portion at breakfast. Top breakfast cereal with sliced bananas, grated apple or a handful of raisins.

Eat dessert first

If your children are too hungry to wait for supper, give them dessert first – apple slices, grapes, melon – to stave off their hunger pangs and help reach their 5-a-day target.

Drink fruit

Fruit smoothies and shakes are a delicious way to get a portion or two of fruit. Liquidise fresh or tinned fruit (such as strawberries, mango or bananas) with fruit juice and/or yoghurt or milk (see recipes for smoothies and shakes on pages 155–157).

SPRINKLE OF SUGAR

If I find strawberries or other summer fruit lacking in flavour, I let my children sprinkle on a little sugar. After a few minutes, the sugar will have dissolved on the fruit surface and brought out a nice flavour.

Q&A

Question: *How can I persuade my children to snack on fruit instead of biscuits?*

Answer: Fruit, cut into bite-sized pieces, will be more attractive than whole fruit for younger children. Make a fruit platter of bite-sized pieces of fruit and let your children dig in.

If your children must snack in front of the television, give them a bowl of grapes, cherries or sliced apples. Without realising it, my daughters often get through a couple of fruit portions while watching their favourite programme.

Make fruit salad together

Let them choose their own fruit combinations. Younger children can peel bananas and satsumas, or prepare grapes; older children can chop and slice plums, apples and peaches.

Keep it varied

Children can easily get bored with the same fruit (such as apples and bananas). Try to eat a different fruit at least once a week. Enjoy the fruits of the seasons by choosing strawberries, raspberries and peaches in the summer, blackberries and plums in the autumn, grapes and clementines in the winter.

Have a dessert

Puddings can be healthy. Try fruit kebabs (threaded onto cocktail sticks or wooden skewers), banana custard, baked apples stuffed with raisins, baked bananas with chocolate (see recipe overleaf), fresh or tinned fruit mixed with yoghurt, rice pudding with stewed apples, dried apricots or fresh raspberries, and apple crumble. See the recipes on pp. 145–148.

Display fruit

If fruit is on display – say in a fruit bowl – in a place your children can easily reach, they're more likely to grab some as they go past.

EATING DRIED FRUIT

Dried fruit is a healthy snack but can stick to the teeth, making it as potentially harmful as sweets. Follow with a drink of water and a small piece of cheese. Or encourage tooth-brushing shortly afterwards.

Make fruit look terrific

When preparing a fruit arrangement or fruit salad, think of colour combinations. Try to contrast two or three different coloured fruit, such as strawberries with bite-sized pieces of Galia melon; blackberries with sliced peaches; mix red and green grapes. Arrange fruit in simple patterns: orange segments in a star shape; alternate plum and nectarine slices; banana slices around the rim of a plate with kiwi slices in the centre. Or let your children make their own patterns.

BAKED BANANAS WITH CHOCOLATE BUTTONS

MAKES 4 SERVINGS

- *4 bananas*
- *Chocolate buttons*

1 *Preheat the oven to 200 °C/400 °F/Gas mark 6.*
2 *Peel the bananas. Make a slit lengthwise in each banana, not quite cutting all the way through.*
3 *Insert the chocolate buttons in the banana slits. Wrap each banana loosely in foil and place on a baking tray.*
4 *Bake in the oven for 15 minutes. Unwrap the foil parcels when cool enough and the bananas will be oozing with delicious chocolate sauce!*

Mix with yoghurt

Mix berries or chopped soft fruit such as bananas with plain or fruit yoghurt. Alternatively, layer chopped or mashed fruit with yoghurt in tall sundae glasses.

Make fruit lollies

Make fruit lollies or 'ice cream' by freezing one of the following mixtures in plastic lolly moulds or little fromage frais pots (insert a wooden lolly stick when half-frozen):

■ Puréed strawberries or mango

■ Mashed raspberries mixed with an equal amount of raspberry yoghurt

■ Mashed banana

FRUIT ACIDS

Fruit contains natural fruit acids, which can over time dissolve the tooth enamel. Serve cheese with fruit at mealtimes or follow eating fruit with a small piece of cheese. Cheese is alkaline and rich in calcium, and neutralises the fruit acids.

Flip a pancake

Not just for Pancake Day. Try filling pancakes with sliced bananas; tinned pineapple; sliced mango; thawed frozen summer fruits; crushed raspberries ... the possibilities are endless (see recipe page 145).

BANANA ICE

Children will enjoy helping to make this ultra-easy 'ice cream', which is a good source of fibre, vitamin C, vitamin B6.
Storage: 3 months in the freezer; do not re-freeze
Preparation: 5 minutes

MAKES 2 CHILD PORTIONS

- *2 ripe bananas*

1 *Peel and mash the bananas. Transfer to a small plastic container. Cover and place in the freezer for several hours.*
2 *Allow it to stand at room temperature for 10 minutes before serving.*
3 *Serve in bowls or in ice cream cones.*

SUGAR IN DISGUISE

Fruit bars and fruit snack rolls are marketed as healthy alternatives to fruit but are far removed from the fresh version and can be very harmful to the teeth. The main ingredients – concentrated fruit juice and puree – are almost pure sugar, and these are supplemented with extra sugar, fruit acids, flavours and colours. Nothing healthy about these. Worse, the bars stick to the teeth, making them just as damaging as sweets.

Summary

- Five portions of fruit and vegetables a day are recommended to help keep children healthy, fight off illnesses and protect them from heart disease and cancer in later life.

- Set a good example – children are more likely to eat fruit and vegetables if they see you enjoying these foods daily and if there's a plentiful supply in the house.

- Don't worry too much if they don't like many vegetables. Stick with the ones they will eat – they can get the key nutrients from extra fruit.

- Unpopular vegetables can often be disguised – in soup, curry, pies, casseroles, pizza toppings or pasta sauce – and then new vegetables gradually introduced with a food they already like.

3 big kids

We've been bombarded by media scare stories about childhood obesity. Hardly a week goes by without a TV programme or newspaper article featuring the plight of obese children. But while such stories often focus on the very overweight, it's easy to overlook the day to day problems faced by 'big' kids. It's even easier to miss the signs in your own family or your friends – after all, you see them every day so any weight change isn't as obvious. Lets face it, no one wants to admit that their own child may be too heavy.

But one in three children under 10 years old are overweight. Contrary to popular belief, most of them don't shed their puppy fat. Six in ten chubby pre-schoolers will be overweight by the time they are 12 years. And overweight teenagers have a 70 per cent chance of becoming an overweight adult.

The earlier you can address the problem the better. It's harder to undo bad eating habits or to instil a regular exercise habit later on.

OVERWEIGHT CHILDREN
Children who are too heavy between the ages of two and five years face a five-times higher risk of being fat as they become a teenager, according to a 2006 US National Institute of Child Health study.

The weight issue

Child obesity is a 'ticking time bomb', according to a 2004 report by the government's Health Select Committee. One in three children aged 2–15 years are overweight (2006), including nearly one in five children who are classed as obese – three times more than 20 years ago. Children's waistlines have expanded by 4 cm (1½ in) – or two clothing sizes – over the past 20 years according to a 2004 East Leeds Primary Care Trust study. Waist size is an important indicator of increased risk of heart disease in adulthood.

Experts are talking about a looming epidemic of obesity, and the Department of Health predict that, by 2010, 1 million children will be obese. According to the National Obesity Forum, if the number of obese children continues to rise, children will have a shorter life expectancy than their parents.

Why does weight matter?

Being chubby is no fun. Apart from being more likely to be teased, bullied and suffer from low self-esteem and self-worth, overweight children are more likely to develop:

- bone and joint problems (due to excess weight)
- breathing problems and asthma
- high blood pressure, high blood cholesterol, type 2 diabetes and artery damage during their teens and early adulthood
- heart disease and stroke in later life.

According to a 2005 study at St George's Medical School, London, carrying even a small amount of excess fat in your early teens can lead to cardiovascular disease. And obese children are up to 20 per cent more likely to develop cancer as adults, according to a 2004 statement from the National Obesity Forum. Children who are obese in their teens are twice as likely to die by the age of 50.

Is your child overweight or obese?

Your child's body mass index (BMI) indicates whether they're a healthy weight. To calculate your child's BMI divide their weight in kg by their height in metres squared.

For example, if a child weighs 35 kg and is 1.25 m tall, their BMI would be 22.4. A BMI higher than normal for their age means they are overweight. To calculate your child's BMI and for an interpretation of the results go to www.weightconcern.org.uk

WHAT IS OBESITY?

Obesity is defined as a level of body fat that is harmful to health. It can be measured by comparing a child's body mass index (BMI) with the population average. Children with a high BMI for their age are 'overweight' (over the 85th percentile) or 'obese' (above the 95th percentile).

AGE	BMI FOR OVERWEIGHT OR OBESE CHILDREN			
	OVERWEIGHT		OBESE	
	BOYS	GIRLS	BOYS	GIRLS
5	17.4	17.1	19.3	19.2
6	17.6	17.3	19.8	19.7
7	17.9	17.8	20.6	20.5
8	18.4	18.3	21.6	21.6
9	19.1	19.1	22.8	22.8
10	19.8	19.9	24.0	24.1
11	20.6	20.7	25.1	25.4
12	21.2	21.7	26.0	26.7
13	21.9	22.6	26.8	27.8

The Big Question: What makes children put on weight?

The reason why children become overweight is simple: they consume more calories than they burn. Unfortunately the reason why they overeat isn't so straightforward.

A child's personality, home life, relationships and lifestyle affect how much and what he or she eats, as well as the amount of daily activity he or she takes. The truth is today's busy lifestyles make it harder for children to follow a healthy diet than 10 years ago.

Why do some children overeat?

■ These days there's an abundance of foods laden with fat, sugar and salt.

■ Snacks are now a staple part of many children's diets. Grazing and snacking rather than eating balanced meals tends to be the norm.

■ Bigger portions and supersize marketing – especially for snacks and fast food – means that many children have lost track of normal portion sizes.

■ Marketing and advertising of fast food and certain snacks is often aimed at children, and influences what they choose to eat. According to a 2006 report by the London School of Economics, children eat more after seeing junk food advertisements, and those watching the most TV are more likely to be overweight.

■ Children now spend more time in front of the television and computer. This means they're less active and watch more adverts tempting them towards unhealthy food. A 2005 *International Journal of Obesity* study found

JUNK FOOD ADVERTISING

Broadcasting regulator, Ofcom, wants to limit the amount of junk food ads that children watch on TV. Since 2007, ads for products high in fat, sugar and salt during programmes targeted at under-16s were banned. But health campaigners and consumer groups want a complete ban on junk food advertising before the 9 pm watershed.

COUCH POTATOES

Children who watch more than two hours of television a day at the weekend risk becoming obese adults (Middlesex Hospital and University College, London, 2006).

Not getting enough sleep is also a big factor. Young children who watch more than eight hours television a week and sleep fewer than ten hours a night are at greatest risk of obesity (University of Glasgow, 2005).

that the amount of TV children watch predicts whether they will go on to become overweight.

- Parents lead busier lives and so have less time to cook. Many find it easier to feed children ready meals and fast food.

- Most children's menus in restaurants offer foods laden with fat, salt and sugar.

- Food and drink in schools is usually poor quality and loaded with fat, sugar and salt. Most children tend to choose fast food and chips for school meals. Many schools have vending machines selling calorie-laden snacks and drinks.

- Changes in family meal patterns mean that children are more likely to eat in front of the television or on the run.

CHOCCIE AND CHIPS

Fast food and sugary and salty snacks can fool children into eating more calories than their body needs. They are 'energy dense', which means they contain a lot of calories for a small amount of food. The Medical Research Council found that a typical fast food meal had more than one and a half times the calories of a similar-sized portion of a traditional British meal.

On the move? Children and exercise

Children lead inactive lives these days, and spend too much time sitting down. The Health Survey of England found that half of all children do not meet their minimum physical activity target (one hour on at least five days each week).

Schools have reduced the time spent on P.E.: Sport England found that only one in three primary-school children receive the recommended two hours of P.E. per week.

Children are now more likely to get driven to school. Twenty years ago, 80 per cent of children walked or cycled to school. Compare this with a mere 5 per cent of children today.

The healthy way to fight obesity

What's the solution? No one wants to see their child on fad diets, ruining their health. But at the same time, you can't sit back and do nothing. The best approach is to encourage a balanced diet and regular physical activity. Talk to your child about healthy eating and exercise, teach by example and guide your child – but at the same time let your child make his or her own decisions about food.

Healthy mind, healthy body: Building self-esteem

If you boost your child's self-esteem and help them feel more positive about themselves they're more likely to make healthier food choices. Make a point of praising their accomplishments, emphasise their strengths, and encourage them to try new skills to foster success. Never call them fat or tell them to lose weight. Let them know that it's what's inside that matters and that you love them for who they are. Play down your concerns about their weight – or even concerns about your own weight.

Don't put a child on a diet

You shouldn't restrict your child's caloric intake without the advice of a dietitian. Nutritional needs during childhood are high and important nutrients that are essential to a child's health could be missed out. Instead make healthy changes to the way they eat. (If you think your child is obese – see your GP, who may advise gradual weight loss under the guidance of a dietitian.)

Eat together

Try to have family meals as often as possible. Eating together allows you to have a positive influence over your children's food choices and the amount of food they eat. A 2005 Australian study found that children who eat regular meals with their family are far less likely to be overweight by the age of 14. They are also less likely to eat unhealthy snacks and more likely to eat well when they are not at home.

Set a good example

Children are more likely to copy what you do than do what you say. They learn a lot about food and activity by watching their parents. They should see that you exercise and eat a balanced diet. Share mealtimes as often as possible and eat the same foods.

Don't use food as a reward

Rewarding good behaviour with sweets only reinforces the idea that they're a special treat and makes children crave them more. Allow them in moderation, say, on one day of the week and at the end of a meal.

DO YOU HAVE WEIGHT WORRIES?

Do you worry about your own weight and shape? Have you regularly dieted or tried to watch your weight? Some experts believe that children's attitudes to food and their body image may be passed down from their parents. Children learn by example. If children see their mother shunning snack foods or counting calories they are likely to do the same. A mother's neurosis about food may rub off on her daughter.

■ A study involving 100 young children concluded that dieting parents or those who are overanxious about food, may be to blame for their children's unhealthy attitude towards eating and their body (Source: Glasgow University).

■ Mothers who dislike body fat are communicating that attitude to their children (Source: St Mary's Hospital, London).

■ Overprotective, uncommunicative parents are more likely to raise children who will develop an eating disorder (Source: Manchester University).

Don't ban any foods

Allow all foods, but explain that certain ones should be eaten only occasionally or kept as special treats. Banning a food increases children's desire for it and makes it more likely that they'll eat it in secret.

Provide healthy snacks

Instead of biscuits, crisps and chocolate make sure there are healthier alternatives to hand at home. Fresh fruit, low-fat yoghurt, wholemeal toast and wholegrain breakfast cereals are good choices. Keep them in a place where your child can easily get at them, for example a fruit bowl on the table or yoghurts at the front of the fridge.

Get them moving

Look for ways to incorporate activity into everything you do, and make this as much fun as possible. Walk or cycle with your children to and from school. Try to increase the amount of exercise you do together as a family – swimming, playing football, a family walk or bike ride. (See Chapter 8: active kids.)

Get tough on telly!

Plan exactly what your children will watch on television and agree on a defined time period. Once the programmes have finished, switch off the television – no matter how much they protest. The American Academy of Paediatrics recommends that children should not watch more than two hours of television a day.

Don't put a TV in your child's bedroom. Psychologists say this distracts children from more active hobbies during the daytime, and sleep at nightime. Keep your child busy with other activities so he or she won't have much time left for sitting in front of the television.

IS YOUR CHILD STRESSED?

Stressed children snack more, eat more fatty food, skip breakfast more often and eat fewer fruits and vegetables, say British researchers. A study of more than 4,000 London schoolchildren aged 11–12 found that the higher the stress levels, the worse a child's diet becomes.

TV TROUBLE

An American study of 6–11-year-olds found that those who watched more than five hours of TV a day were more than four times as likely to be overweight as those who watched two hours or less a day.

Researchers have shown that children burn fewer calories watching television than if they were reading or drawing a picture! TV watching induces an almost trance-like state in children, reducing their energy output to a bare minimum.

Watching TV for an extra two hours a day increases the chances of obesity by 25 per cent.

tip *A third of all new cases of obesity could be prevented by taking a half-hour walk every day.*

Balance activity and viewing time

Let the number of hours of exercise your children take equal the number of hours of television they're allowed to watch. If they've done an hour's physical activity during the day, you could allocate an hour's television watching.

Don't snack and view

Discourage your children from eating meals or unhealthy snacks while watching television. Because their mind will be on the television and not on the food, they won't notice when they're full up or no longer hungry. They tend to eat more while watching TV – up to a quarter of their daily food intake, according to a 2004 study at Stanford University, USA.

Make exercise fun

Encourage children to pick activities they enjoy – having fun is the key to exercising for life. Provide plenty of play equipment at home – hoppers, balls, trampolines, basketball rings, scooters, bikes and skipping ropes. Introduce them to the wide range of sports available – football, informal racket games, gymnastics, dance lessons, trampolining and swimming. For older children, athletics, roller skating, hockey, tennis, badminton, netball, jogging and sailing are also great fun. (See Chapter 8: active kids.)

Eat and stay slim: healthy rules for your child (and the rest of the family)

- Follow the one-third rule – vegetables should fill at least one third of the plate. This will help satisfy your child's hunger as well as provide essential nutrients.

- Check serving sizes – the more food you put on children's plates, the more they eat, according to a 2005 study at Cornell University, USA. Try cutting portion sizes of high calorie foods and increasing portion sizes of lower calorie veggies and fruits.

- Aim for five portions of fruit and vegetables a day.

- Swap sugary and fizzy drinks for lower sugar versions (e.g. fruit juice diluted half and half with water) or, ideally, water. One 330 ml can of drink contains on average 35 g (7 teaspoons) of sugar – equivalent to five lollipops.

- Always eat food sitting at a table – eating in front of the TV or on the run makes you consume more because you don't concentrate fully.

- Give them fruit to take to school for break times – such as apples, satsumas and grapes.

- Don't ditch dairy products in a bid to save calories: switch to low-fat or skimmed versions. They contain just as much calcium.

- Offer brown rather than white carbohydrates – wholegrain bread, bran cereals and wholewheat pasta are rich in fibre, which makes your child feel fuller. Switch gradually, though, to avoid stomach upsets.

- Don't ban chocolate – for treats, offer a fun-sized chocolate bar.

- Have soup made with lots of veggies more often – it's filling, low in calories and nutritious. Your children can help make it, or you can buy ready-made fresh versions.

- Make chips healthier by thickly slicing potatoes and baking them in the oven, tossed in a little olive oil (see recipe on page 51).

- Include fruit for desserts – fresh fruit, stewed apples or pears with custard, baked apples and fruit crumble.

- Encourage your child to eat slowly and enjoy every mouthful. Teach by example.

FIT FOR LIFE: HOW MUCH EXERCISE SHOULD CHILDREN GET?

6–10-year-olds: 60 minutes of moderate intensity activity as part of their lifestyle every day. It doesn't have to be done in one go.

11–15-year-olds: 30–60 minutes of moderate to vigorous activity every day as part of their lifestyle. Plus three sessions per week of continuous vigorous activity lasting at least 20 minutes, e.g. jogging, swimming, cycling, dancing or football.

For both age groups, this recommendation can include everyday activities such as walking, unstructured play such as ball games, 'chase' and hide and seek, sports activities and P.E.

- Start the day with porridge – oats keep your child fuller for longer and keep cravings at bay.

- Include baked beans and lentils in meals – they're filling, nutritious and don't cause a rapid rise in blood sugar, which means they provide longer-lasting energy.

- Encourage your child to drink at least six glasses of fluid a day. Thirst is sometimes mistaken for hunger. Swap squash and sugary drinks for water with a twist of lemon or lime.

Q&A

Question: How can I avoid mealtimes becoming a battleground?

Answer: Conflicts over food are very common. But you can keep mealtimes as stress-free as possible. Don't comment on how much your child eats. Avoid discussing your child's weight or eating habits at the table. Involve him or her in planning the meal and, if they wish, preparing and serving the meal. For example, ask them which vegetables they would prefer ('shall we have cauliflower or broccoli?'), provide a guided choice ('would you prefer minestrone or tomato soup?'; 'would you like baked beans or tuna and sweetcorn with your jacket potato?').

Q&A

Question: My child has a big appetite – should I restrict the amount she eats?

Answer: At mealtimes, let her fill up with nutritious foods that contain lots of fibre and water – vegetable dishes, salads, jacket potatoes, wholemeal pasta, fresh fruit and baked apples. If your child is still hungry after the meal, offer her more food, but only the healthy kind – fresh fruit, vegetables and yoghurt, for example. Resist giving in to demands for unhealthy snacks. Contrary to popular belief, sugary and salty snacks don't fill children up or satisfy their appetite – they can even have the opposite effect, stimulating their taste buds to want more and increasing their thirst for more sugary drinks. It takes time for a child – or indeed an adult – to get used to eating different types and amounts of food.

OVEN POTATO WEDGES

These are a real treat for children. They're healthier than chips as they're lower in fat and, with the skins left on, they retain much of their vitamin C.

MAKES 4 SERVINGS

- *4 medium potatoes, scrubbed (adjust the quantity according to your children's appetite)*
- *4 tsp (20 ml) sunflower or olive oil*
- *Optional: garlic powder; Parmesan cheese; chilli powder*

1 *Pre-heat the oven to 200°C/400°F/Gas mark 6.*
2 *Cut each potato lengthways, then cut each half into 6 wedges.*
3 *Place in a baking tin and turn in the oil until each piece is lightly coated.*
4 *Bake for 35–40 minutes turning occasionally until the potatoes are soft inside and golden brown on the outside.*
5 *Sprinkle on one of the optional ingredients 5 minutes before the end of cooking.*

Summary

- Build your children's self-esteem and make them feel valued – they'll be more likely to make healthier food and activity choices.

- Don't put your child on a diet – instead talk about healthy eating.

- Teach by example – they should see that you exercise and eat a balanced diet.

- Don't ban any food – it'll only increase your child's desire for it.

- Get them moving – encourage active interests, walk or cycle with your children to and from school and exercise together as a family.

4 tricky little customers

Easy ways to feed fussy eaters

It can be frustrating trying to feed children who refuse to eat proper meals. You worry about them not getting enough calories, becoming malnourished and, as a result, more vulnerable to illness and infection.

- The first thing to remember is that children don't voluntarily starve themselves: they're programmed for survival! As long as there's food available, children will make sure they get enough.

- Secondly, some children are very good at using food to wind up their parents. The more firmly they refuse to finish their plate at mealtimes, the more attention they get. They know that refusing food results in attention.

Young children

Most children go through phases of fussy eating. From as early as their second year, they start to get clear opinions about what they will and won't eat, loving a certain food one day and disliking it the next.

They quickly realise that food is one area where they have control. Refusing a particular food is a way of asserting their independence and gaining attention. The more firmly they reject a particular food, the more attention they get and a vicious circle is soon established. Mealtimes then present the perfect opportunity to test the boundaries.

Older children

Fussy eating isn't just confined to the toddler years. Faddy eating habits often persist for many years – and children don't always just 'grow out of them'. The earlier you tackle the issue, the better. With older children it just takes more perseverance.

Happy Eaters: Making mealtimes easier

Children need to be trained to eat proper meals and nutritious food. You don't have to insist that they clear their plate but you need to set your own rules.

A clear strategy will help to persuade your child that food is enjoyable and fun. Ultimately, it will help your child to develop greater confidence around food.

Tips for Tots: Try these solutions for fussy eaters

Get them in the kitchen

Encourage your children to help with the shopping and preparing meals. This will increase their interest in the food, and they'll be more likely to eat the meal if they've been involved in making it.

Be a good role model

Children learn by example so let them see that you enjoy eating healthy meals. They're also more likely to eat foods that they've seen you eat. Have meals together whenever possible – ideally once a day, otherwise at least once a week – and show them you enjoy trying new tastes. Serve your children the same food as everyone else.

Build up their appetite

Ensure they've taken plenty of fresh air and exercise; they do wonders for the appetite. It's amazing how less fussy children become if they are really hungry!

Let children serve themselves

Put the food in dishes in the centre of the table so everyone can serve himself or herself. By the age of four years most children can judge how much they can eat. You'll also be helping them become more socially aware and independent, allowing them to make their own choices and take responsibility for their actions. My youngest daughter used to refuse bread with margarine. Once I put the bread and margarine out separately on the table, she helped herself to the margarine, spreading on the amount she wanted! Since then, she eats bread with margarine with the rest of the family.

Q&A

Question: How can I be sure that my daughter isn't starving herself when she eats so little at mealtimes?

Answer: She may be eating more than you think. Does she have snacks between meals or lots of drinks? These can amount to a large proportion of a child's daily food intake. When children consistently refuse meals, many parents are only too pleased for their child to eat something (even if it's a biscuit) rather than nothing. So it's tempting to give in to demands for snacks.

Snacks aren't necessarily a bad thing, provided they supply nutrients in proportion to their energy content. But if your daughter is filling up on biscuits, soft drinks and crisps she won't be getting the vitamins, minerals and fibre she needs. She'll be satisfying her hunger with 'empty' calories and have little appetite left for nutritious food. Follow the advice below on how to encourage proper meals.

MOTHER'S FOOD TASTES SHAPE CHILDREN'S TASTES

According to a 2002 US study, mothers influence the food likes and dislikes of their children as early as the age of two years through their own food preferences. If you don't like a food, you are less likely to offer it to your children. But it is worth making the effort to introduce your children to new tastes even if you are not keen on the food yourself – kids are more likely to accept new foods before the age of eight years.

Q&A

Question: What should I do when my fussy eater absolutely insists on snacks between meals?

Answer: Give your child no more than two snacks a day – the first between breakfast and lunch and the second between lunch and tea. There should be no extra snacks if he refuses his meal. Suitable snacks could be fresh fruit (such as sliced apples, bananas, grapes or kiwi fruit), cheese, wholemeal crackers, small wholemeal sandwiches or a carton of yoghurt. No matter how much he protests or requests unhealthy snacks, stand firm and don't give him any other food. It will be tough at first – no parent wants to 'starve' their child – but after a week or so he'll soon get the message that the best thing to do at mealtimes is to eat.

Think small

Even if the portion seems ridiculously tiny to you, it's better that your child eats a small amount of everything than nothing at all. A big pile of food on the plate can be off-putting for young children. As a rule of thumb, the younger the child, the smaller the pieces of food – try tiny broccoli florets, small squares of toast, super-thin apple slices.

Keep mealtimes happy

Meals should be enjoyable. Don't discuss eating behaviour, negative food or family issues at mealtimes. Try to achieve a relaxed atmosphere – keep conversation light and fun.

Play with food

You can encourage fussy eaters, especially younger children, to eat good food by presenting it imaginatively. Arrange food in simple shapes, say a circle, a star, a face or a train, or try playing games – such as the train (broccoli) going into the tunnel (mouth)!

Don't get cross

If your child refuses the meal or certain foods, keep your temper. Explain that you expect them to try it and don't offer an alternative. You need to be patient but persistent – not easy, I know, especially when you've spent time preparing a meal. Refusing food loses its appeal if you don't react. (This approach has stretched my patience to the limit, but at the age of six years, my youngest daughter now understands that the best thing to do at mealtimes is to eat!)

Don't force feed

You can't make a child eat – he or she will react to your concern and will be even less likely to eat the food. Most adults have bad memories of being made to eat a particular food as a child – remember school dinners? – and then hating it ever since!

Don't bargain with food

It's tempting to say – 'no pudding unless you've eaten your vegetables'. But never promise children a favourite food or dessert only when they've finished their main course – this will only reinforce the dislike of the refused food and make the other food seem more special. It's reasonable to expect them to try everything, so you could ask them to have, say, two sprouts, as a compromise. This will seem less daunting.

Keep trying!

If a food is rejected, it doesn't mean they'll never eat it. Children's tastes do change over time. Keep re-introducing those foods they reject, say once a fortnight or once a month, and don't make a fuss. It can take up to 8–10 attempts to get a child to eat a new food. Don't reinforce their dislike of a particular food by telling everyone else that your child won't eat, say, tomatoes or whatever. He'll be even less likely to try it again.

Give them options

Encourage children to select their own food but from within a limited choice, e.g. 'would you like beans or peas with that?' rather than 'would you like vegetables?'

Set a time limit

If they refuse to eat the meal within, say, 30 minutes, remove it without fuss and don't offer any other food until next mealtime. Be consistent and remember that they won't become malnourished straight away.

Be strict with snacks

If they don't eat their meal, don't let them fill up on snacks later. Eating between meals will simply take away their appetite for more nutritious foods at mealtimes and perpetuate their taste for salty, sugary processed foods (*see* Q&A on page 56: *What should I do when my fussy eater absolutely insists on snacks between meals?*). If they're genuinely hungry, offer only nutritious food – such as fruit, cheese, yoghurt or nuts.

Eating on the move

It's all too easy to get into the habit of feeding your children on the go – in the car or on other transport – or in front of the television. The problem is children won't learn how to eat proper meals and will miss out on the social benefits of eating together. And it will also be harder to break the habit later on. Try to organise the family routine so that children eat at the table most of the time.

Summary

■ Try to worry less – children won't voluntarily starve themselves.

■ Remember, fussy eaters use food as a way of controlling their surroundings, asserting their independence and gaining attention.

■ It's essential to have a clear strategy at mealtimes.

■ Involve children with menu planning, shopping and the meal preparation whenever possible.

■ Set a good example and try to eat together regularly.

■ Keep mealtimes happy and avoid confrontations over food.

■ Don't get cross or force your children to eat something they dislike.

■ Don't bargain with food.

■ Children's tastes change over time – keep re-introducing foods.

■ Don't allow snacks later if they don't eat their meal.

5 how to survive shopping with the children

'Mum, can I have. . .?'

Supermarket shopping with kids in tow can be fraught with problems. Manufacturers know that children are attracted by bright, fun packaging, cartoon characters and on-pack promotions rather than what's inside. These are all successful marketing ploys to get children to persuade their parents to buy what they want. And the products that appeal most to children are invariably packed with fat, sugar, salt or artificial additives. It's vital to develop a clear strategy to combat pester power when food shopping. Otherwise it can quickly turn into a battle of wills.

Survival tactics

Make a shopping list. . .

. . .and then buy only what's on the list! Having already made your shopping decisions at home, your children will have less time to become distracted by packaging and you have the perfect excuse: 'It's not on the list this week.'

You're in charge!

Remember your children can't actually make you buy anything: you have to decide to buy it! If your children pester you, don't be drawn into an argument. Explain calmly why you won't buy the product and stand firm. It's not easy, but if you're consistent each time you go shopping, the message will get through.

Avoid tired and hungry moments

Try to schedule shopping when neither you nor the children are vulnerable. They'll be less likely to pester – and you'll be less likely to give in – if you can avoid shopping straight after school, in the evening or just before a meal.

Skip the 'danger' zones

Steer a route through the supermarket avoiding the aisles with the sweets, crisps and fizzy drinks. Where there's less temptation. . .

Check labels

To judge the quality of the food you buy for your children, look at the nutrition information panel on food packages.

Companies that label foods clearly make it easier for you to make healthier choices when buying food. There are two labelling systems in use at present:

1 The government-backed traffic light colour-coded labelling uses a red, amber or green symbol to signal whether foods contain high, medium or low levels of fat, saturated fat, sugar and salt.

2 The system of Guideline Daily Amounts (GDAs) gives the amount of calories, fat, saturated fat, sugar and salt in a serving plus the percentage of the GDA.

Traffic light labelling

Waitrose, Sainsbury's, the Co-op and some other stores have put traffic light labels on the front of some of their products. Each use their own designs and, although they look different, the red, amber or green should mean exactly the same on their products.

Traffic light colours tell you whether the food has high, medium or low amounts of each of these nutrients in 100 g of the food. They can help you choose between products and keep a check on the high-fat, high-sugar and high-salt foods you eat.

Many of the foods with traffic light colours will have a mixture of red, amber and greens. The idea is, when you're choosing between similar products, to go for more greens (low) and ambers (medium), and fewer reds (high).

GDA labelling

GDA labelling allows you to check how the nutrient content *in a serving of food* fits into a child's (or adult's) overall daily diet. Kellogg's, Danone, Kraft, Nestlé, PepsiCo and other companies use GDA labelling on packaging instead of traffic light labelling. These companies say that customers prefer straight nutritional facts to colour coding and that traffic light labelling is misleading (healthy foods such as olive oil and nuts have a red light).

A serving of Kellogg's cornflakes, for example, contains 112 calories, or 6 per cent of the GDA.

What are guideline daily amounts (GDAs)?

GDAs are a guide to how much energy (calories) and the amount of key nutrients you should consume each day for a healthy diet.

They are guidelines for an average person or child with a healthy weight and an average level of activity. Individual requirements will differ, depending on your body weight, age, the amount of exercise you do and whether you are still growing. GDAs were developed by food manufacturers and retailers. They are published by the Institute of Grocery Distribution (IGD): a food and grocery industry research organisation.

There are two ways that you can use GDA information:

1 To keep an eye on what you are eating. For example, if you are concerned about fat intake, you can see how much of your fat GDA is taken up by a particular food, and then use the GDAs on other foods to opt for lower fat foods during the rest of the day. (For each GDA your total should add up to around 100 per cent).

2 Use the GDA information to compare foods.

GDAS FOR GIRLS				
	4–6 YEARS	7–10 YEARS	11–14 YEARS	15–18 YEARS
Energy (kcal)	1550	1750	1850	2100
Fat (g)	60	70	70	80
Saturated fat (g)	20	20	25	25
Carbohydrate (g)	195	220	230	265
Total sugars (g)*	75	85	90	105
Protein (g)	20	28	42	55
Fibre (g)	12	16	20	24
Salt (g)	3	5	6	6

* includes added sugars and naturally occurring sugars such as those found in fruit, fruit juice and milk

GDAS FOR BOYS				
	4–6 YEARS	7–10 YEARS	11–14 YEARS	15–18 YEARS
Energy (kcal)	1700	1950	2200	2750
Fat (g)	65	75	85	105
Saturated fat (g)	20	25	25	35
Carbohydrate (g)	215	245	275	345
Total sugars (g)*	85	100	110	140
Protein (g)	20	28	41	45
Fibre (g)	12	16	20	24
Salt (g)	3	5	6	6

* includes added sugars and naturally occurring sugars such as those found in fruit, fruit juice and milk

WHAT'S A LOT OR A LITTLE?		
	A lot per 100 g	A little per 100 g
Sugars	10 g	2.0 g
Total fat	20 g	3.0 g
Saturated fat	5.0 g	1.0 g
Fibre	3.0 g	0.5 g
Sodium	0.5 g	0.1 g
Salt	1.25 g	0.25 g

Source: Food Standards Agency

Nutritional information

You will also see a panel on food labels giving the nutritional breakdown of the food per 100 g (or 100 ml). You may also see amounts per serving, but this must be in addition to the 100 g or 100 ml breakdown.

Looking at the nutrients per 100 g helps you compare levels of nutrients in different products. Here's a guide to the nutrients you'll see listed on the nutrition labels.

Energy

This is the amount of energy that the food will give you. It is measured either in calories (kcal) or joules (kJ).

Protein

Protein provides the building material for the body and is essential for growth and repair. Protein-rich foods include meat, fish, poultry, milk and dairy foods, eggs, beans, lentils and nuts.

Carbohydrates

Carbohydrates provide fuel for the body. They include simple carbohydrates/sugars (found in, for example, fruit, biscuits and drinks) and complex carbohydrates/starch (found in, for example, potatoes, bread, pasta and rice).

Simple carbohydrates are often listed on food labels as 'Carbohydrates (of which sugars)'. This includes added sugars and the natural sugars found in fruit and milk. The total figure for carbohydrates on food labels includes starch and sugars.

Fats

Fat provides more than twice as many calories as carbohydrate or protein so eating too much of it can lead to weight gain. Children need some fat in their diet to keep healthy (it supplies energy, essential fatty acids, and helps absorb vitamins A, D and E). Many food labels give the product's total fat content. Some food labels also break the figures down into these different types of fat: saturates, monounsaturates and polyunsaturates.

Saturated fat can raise blood cholesterol levels, which increases the chance of developing heart disease. Monounsaturates and polyunsaturates are both types of unsaturated fat. These don't raise blood cholesterol in the same way as saturated fats and provide us with the essential fatty acids that the body needs.

Dietary fibre

Fibre helps to keep the gut healthy and prevent constipation and bowel problems. Good sources include wholegrain breakfast cereal, beans, lentils, nuts, wholemeal bread, fruit and vegetables.

Salt and sodium

Salt is made up of sodium and chloride. Sodium is essential for fluid balance in the body but eating too much can raise blood pressure. Salt is often listed as sodium on food labels (salt = sodium × 2.5).

Ingredients list

To get a feel for whether a product is high in a certain ingredient, you might need to look at the ingredients list. Ingredients lists always start with the biggest ingredient first and are listed in descending order of weight. For example, if sugar appears among the first ingredients you know that the food contains high levels of sugar.

Seek out the sugar

Sugar can be hard to spot in children's food as it's called so many different things. Check labels for names such as sucrose, glucose syrup, invert sugar syrup, fructose, dextrose, maltodextrin, fruit syrup and glucose. They're all forms of sugar and all can be harmful to teeth.

Look for other ingredients that can be used to add sweetness – fruit juice, concentrated fruit juice, honey, golden syrup and sweetened condensed milk. They can still damage teeth.

RECOGNISE THE TRICKS OF THE TRADE THAT MAKE PRODUCTS ATTRACTIVE TO CHILDREN

Cartoon characters on food packages are designed to grab children's attention and make you buy the product. But many of these types of products are unhealthy and consist of low-quality ingredients.

What you can do: Look at the ingredients and nutrition label and explain to your children what's wrong with the contents – 'too much sugar or salt' for example. With older children, encourage them to try and find out for themselves – they'll enjoy the challenge – and let them come to their own (and, hopefully, the right) conclusions.

Be strict about on-pack promotions – collectable free gifts or cheap offers for toys and gadgets will appeal to children.

What you can do: Look carefully at what's in the product before you agree to buy it. If it's a product you'd rather not buy, stand firm and steer your children towards healthier choices.

By encouraging token collection for school books, computer equipment and membership to clubs, or providing interactive websites, manufacturers encourage brand loyalty. This is fine if it's a healthy product, otherwise this ploy pressurises you to buy products you wouldn't otherwise want for your children.

What you can do: Check whether the number of tokens required is realistic (how many products would you need to buy to earn enough tokens?) and whether they really do offer good value for money.

Children love foods that come in novelty shapes, textures and sizes – anything that makes food easy and fun to eat. Great if it's a healthy product – such as fun-sized cheese portions or squeezy yoghurt pots – but many novelty products are high in sugar, fat or salt (as well as being expensive).

What you can do: Save money by making your own healthy novelty food. Chop vegetables or potatoes into fun shapes, cut small cubes of cheese, serve food in fun dishes, and place healthy snacks like nuts in tiny pots.

Get wise to hydrogenated fat

This processed fat is an artificially saturated fat and contains trans fats (or trans fatty acids), which are a serious health risk. They increase blood levels of LDL ('bad') cholesterol and risk of heart disease, stroke, diabetes and some types of cancer. There is no safe limit, according to the US Institute of Medicine. The UK Food Standards Agency recommends you keep your intake to a minimum. As a result of pressure from health campaigners, many food companies are removing hydrogenating fats from their foods and replacing them with palm oil or butter. You won't see trans fats on food labels but you should look out for hydrogenated or partially hydrogenated fats on food labels. Cut down on these:

- Spreads made with hydrogenated oils. A good alternative is olive oil spread.

- Fast food. Most is fried in partially hydrogenated oil.

- Cakes and biscuits. More hydrogenated fat and shortening (high in trans fats) are used in these than any other food. Opt for biscuits made with butter instead.

- Crisps and snacks.

- Chocolate bars. The vegetable fat on the label means hydrogenated fat.

Q&A

Question: Is it better to buy children's foods that have added vitamins?

Answer: By adding extra vitamins to a basically unhealthy product, such as a sugary drink, a sugary processed cereal or a packet of sweets, manufacturers know that parents are more likely to buy it. But this doesn't turn an inherently unhealthy product into a good one. Vitamin-enriched sweets or biscuits are still high in sugar and bad for children's teeth. If you wouldn't have bought the product without vitamins, don't buy it now.

Spot the additives

Additives are supposed to be safe in theory. But they may provoke an allergic reaction in some children. They're present in up to three-quarters of children's food, according to a survey by Organix. As a result, children could end up eating huge amounts of additives by the time they reach their teens. Sweets, savoury snacks, desserts and snack bars are the worst offenders.

A government-funded study at the UK's Asthma and Allergy Research Centre found that certain food colours and preservatives cause hyperactive behaviour in as many as one in four young children. They recommended that all children (not only hyperactive children) would benefit from the removal of artificial food colourings from their diet. These are the additives to look out for on food labels:

Colours:
Tartrazine (E102)
Sunset Yellow (E110)
Carmoisine (E122)
Ponceau 4R (E124)

Preservative:
Sodium Benzoate (E211)

Q&A

Question: How can I stop my children nagging me for sweets and chocolates displayed at the checkout?

Answer: It is infuriating that many supermarkets display sweets and snacks at their checkouts, on aisle ends or in dump-bins near the tills. Such tempting displays are deliberately placed to activate pester power and increase sales. Here's what you can do:

- Try to avoid shops that sell sweets at the checkout. (Asda is committed to substituting confectionery with healthy snacks and fruit and vegetables at its checkouts.)

- Tell supermarkets what you think – write to the manager of the store.

- Join the 'Chuck Sweets off the Checkout!' campaign run by the Parents' Jury of the Food Commission (www.parentsjury.org.uk).

Summary

- Avoid doing the shopping when you and the children are tired or hungry.

- Make a shopping list – and then buy only what's on the list. Remember you're in charge – the children can't make you buy anything you don't want.

- Be sensible. Don't encourage your children to choose which product they want if it's one you'd actually rather they didn't eat at all!

- Recognise the tricks of the trade that make products attractive to children.

- Look at the labels and explain to children what's wrong with the contents.

- Check labels for hidden sugar, hydrogenated fat and artificial additives.

6   healthy eating at school

In recent years, bad eating habits have been a routine part of the school day. Spending on food for school dinners can be as low as 37p per child, with money being saved by dishing up cheap, processed foods. The government is aiming to see this amount rise to 50p per child in primary schools and 60p in secondary schools.

What's being done?

The Scottish Executive has already introduced higher standards for school meals and committed £63.5m over three years to improvements. The Welsh Assembly has also put extra money on children's plates. In England, a School Food Trust (funded by the Department for Education and Skills and the Lottery Fund) has been set up to work with schools and parents to improve meals. School food is also to become part of the OFSTED inspections.

The additional funding has also been earmarked to provide training and an increase in work hours for school cooks.

A little bit of history. . .

- School meals first became a national issue in 1906 when the Liberal government introduced the Education (Provision of Meals) Act. By 1920 over a million children received school meals.

- Free school milk was introduced in 1924 (and was withdrawn by the government in the early 1970s).

- By 1947 the full cost of school meals was met by the government. But this 100 per cent grant was withdrawn in 1967 and parents had to contribute.

- In 1978 the government halved their spending on school meals – this immediately reduced the quality of the meals and service. Cafeterias were introduced into secondary schools.

- The 1980 Education Act gave LEA's the power to axe school meals. It also got rid of minimum nutritional standards and the fixed price 'national charge'. Catering was put out to tender and convenience foods, crisps, chips, etc. entered the school menu.

- The School Food Trust was set up in 2005 with £15m of funding from the Department for Education and Skills (DfES) to promote the education and health of children and young people by improving the quality of food in schools.

- In September 2006 the Department for Education introduced new food standards.

- The government has earmarked an extra £240m to subsidise healthy ingredients until 2011 and school cooks will receive extra training.

Why is healthy school food so important?

- Parents want their children to have the best possible start in life – and a healthy diet is an important part of that.

- School food has an important role to play in developing pupils' social and personal attitudes and behaviours around food.

- Learning about healthy eating at school and home, as well as keeping more active, can help tackle the problem of child obesity.

- An improvement in school meals results in improved behaviour and academic attainment.

What's on the menu?

All schools should offer a balanced meal each day and must provide a lunch for children entitled to free school meals.

There are rules about what schools should be providing for lunch. In September 2006 the Department for Education introduced new food standards to improve pupils' health, behaviour and concentration. These guidelines are based on recommendations of the School Meals Review Panel report, 'Turning the Tables: Transforming School Food' (2005), and follow a campaign by TV chef Jamie Oliver to improve the quality of school meals.

SCHOOL MEAL GUIDELINES

- No fewer than two servings per day of fruit and vegetables.

- Oily fish should be served at least once every three weeks.

- Bread should be available every day.

- Free, fresh drinking water should be available.

- Salt should not be available at lunch, and ketchup and mayonnaise should only be available in sachets.

- No more than two portions of deep-fried foods in a single week.

- Manufactured meat products, such as chicken nuggets, may only be served occasionally and only providing they meet minimum standards for meat content.

- The only savoury snacks available at lunchtime should be nuts and seeds with no added salt, fat or sugar.

(School Food Trust, 2006)

What food is banned in school meals?

The government has banned the following foods from schools in England from September 2006:

- burgers and sausages from 'meat slurry' and 'mechanically recovered meat'

- sweets (including chewing gum, liquorice, mints, toffees, fruit pastilles and marsh mallows)

- chocolate and chocolate biscuits

- bagged snacks such as crisps, tortilla chips, salted nuts, onion rings and rice crackers.

Primary schools

Most primary schools offer one or two meal choices each day. Your school should be able to tell you about what's on the menu each day, whether there is a choice, how healthier options are promoted and how lunchtimes are managed.

Secondary schools

Secondary schools tend to offer a wider choice of meals but these must still meet key standards for healthy eating. One of the biggest challenges is to encourage pupils to choose healthier options, by making them more appealing and educating children about the benefits of healthier eating. Your school should be able to tell you about the food it offers, what's on the menu each day and how they are promoting healthy eating.

What parents can do

- Ask your child's teacher or the head what food and drink is being provided at school or what your child should be learning about food.

- Monitor the school's meals and ask whether they are meeting the national nutritional standards.

- If you would like to see changes made, talk to the head (or school governors) explaining your concerns.

- Get the school to set up a School Nutritional Action Group (see next page and www.healthedtrust.com) if there isn't one already.

- Talk to other parent–teacher groups to increase pressure and share ideas.

- Cook with your children at home and help them to learn about new foods and flavours.

- Talk to your children about what they eat and drink at school, what food is on offer and what they have learned about food.

- Sit down to eat together at mealtimes, and teach your children good mealtime behaviour.

To find out more, see www.feedmebetter.com.

Set up a School Nutrition Action Group (SNAG)

If your school doesn't already have one, speak to the head about setting up a School Nutrition Action Group (SNAG). This is a school-based alliance involving staff, pupils and caterers, supported by health and education professionals. The idea is that everyone works together to review and expand the range of food and drink available in order to increase the uptake of a healthier diet and ensure consistent messages from the curriculum and the food service.

For information about SNAG activities in schools around the country, see www.healthedtrust.com/pages/snag.htm.

Develop a school food policy

The School Food Trust recommends that every school should have an integrated Whole School Food Policy, preferably reflected in its single School Plan. A school Food Policy is a shared philosophy on all aspects of food and drink that demonstrates how the school cares for and makes a positive contribution to the health and well-being of the pupils.

It should set out a coordinated approach to food and drink to increase the availability of healthier options. The policy should also ensure that all aspects of food and drink are brought together clearly, and coherently, including the taught curriculum, extra-curricular activities, breakfast, tuck shop, school lunch, and consumption of food and drink at school (e.g. pupils bringing in food for break).

For advice on developing a Food Policy in your school, see the guide 'Establishing a Whole School Food Policy', included in the Food in Schools Toolkit developed by the Department of Health/ Department for Education and Skills at http://foodinschools.datacenta.uk.net/. See also 'The Chips are Down: a guide to food policy in schools' by the Health Education Trust (www.healthedtrust.com/pages/chips.htm).

WHAT SHOULD CHILDREN KNOW?

A number of subjects include food in the syllabus and help to educate children about nutrition, digestion, food preparation, cooking and food production.

During Key Stage 1 (5–7 years) children learn that food comes from plants and animals and understand that we must eat a wide variety of food to grow and be healthy.

During Key Stage 2 (7–11 years) children should gain a greater understanding of food, health and hygiene and learn to cook simple dishes.

During Key Stages 3 and 4 (11–16 years) children should develop a more thorough awareness of nutrition, health, food safety and food preparation, learn what constitutes a healthy diet and how to make healthy choices.

From 2008, secondary-school pupils will also be offered cookery lessons. The voluntary course will comprise 24 one-hour lessons, at the end of which pupils will receive a certificate.

Healthy vending machines

Whether or not to have vending machines on school premises is a decision that is made by the head teacher and school's governors. Vending machines are a convenient way to provide drinks and snacks for pupils' choice but they should contain products that help promote the messages taught in the curriculum.

Healthier vending should reflect the objectives of your whole school Food Policy and provide a range of food and drink that is in line with healthier eating and is supportive of a whole school approach.

Since September 2006, school vending machines were no longer allowed to sell chocolates, crisps or sugary fizzy drinks.

For guidance on establishing a healthy drinks vending service, see 'Vending Healthy Drinks: A guide for schools' developed by the Food Standards Agency and Health Education Trust, available at http://www.food.gov.uk/multimedia/pdfs/vendingmachinebooklet.pdf.

See also *Think Healthy Vending* available at http://www.cmo.wales.gov.uk/content/work/schools/vend-book-eng.pdf. The Health Education Trust's Real Choice initiative provides guidance for schools and vending operators. For more information see http://www.healthedtrust.com. Eligible Vending Operators can register with the Health Education Trust to adopt the Real Choice School vending criteria.

THE SCHOOL FRUIT AND VEGETABLE SCHEME

Under the School Fruit and Vegetable Scheme, all four- to six-year-old children in LEA-maintained infant, primary and special schools are entitled to a free piece of fruit or vegetable each school day. This scheme is part of the government's five-a-day programme to increase fruit and vegetable consumption.

Children are offered a choice of apples, pears, bananas, easy-peel citrus fruit such as satsumas, carrots and tomatoes. For more information, see www.5aday.nhs.uk/sfvs/default.aspx.

Healthy tuck shops

A healthier tuck shop can encourage healthier eating and drinking habits at school as well as generating a small income for the school.

Ideally, the healthier tuck shop should be incorporated into your School Food Policy (see page 75) and seen as part of the whole school approach to food and drink provision through the day.

It is important to set up a tuck shop planning group with a project leader and consult the school community early on. It could include pupils, teachers and parents and should have the support of the head. The choice of what to sell should be decided by the School Council or SNAG after consultation with pupils, teachers and parents.

What should I encourage my children to eat for school lunch?

While many schools now offer healthier options, the challenge is encouraging children to choose them. Here are a few guidelines:

HEALTHIER OPTIONS	AVOID
Main course:	
Chicken or fish dishes (but not fried)	Burgers
Baked beans or bean hotpots	Sausages
Vegetable, chicken or lentil soup	Chicken nuggets
Pizza and pasta dishes with tomato or vegetable-based sauces	Pies
Chicken, turkey or vegetable curries	Fish in batter
Jacket potatoes filled with tuna, baked beans, cheese or coleslaw	Pasta dishes with creamy or oily sauces
Vegetable bakes and hotpots	Anything that appears excessively oily, e.g. chilli, Bolognese sauce
Accompaniments:	
Potatoes – boiled, mashed or jacket	Chips
Vegetables – at least one portion of vegetables or salad	Roast potatoes
Dessert:	
Fresh fruit (at least three times a week)	Cookies
Fruit-based puddings, e.g. fruit crumble, banana custard	Cakes
Yoghurt	Sponge puddings
Milk-based pudding, e.g. rice pudding	Roly poly/suet
Drinks:	
Water	Fizzy drinks
Fruit juice	Fruit drinks, squash and soft drinks
Milk	Sugar-free and 'diet' drinks

7 packing a healthy lunch box

It's a daily challenge: who doesn't struggle for inspiration on what to put into their child's lunch box each morning? Who doesn't wonder whether the food they're giving their child for lunch provides enough nutrients? And what parent doesn't suspect that it may come home uneaten anyway?

The main things to remember are that a healthy lunch box should be enjoyable, filling and provide enough energy to sustain your children over several hours of work and play.

And it doesn't have to break the bank. The key to keeping children interested in lunch is variety. Avoid basic sandwiches every day, and keep treats such as crisps and cakes down to a minimum. Instead pack a variety of interesting foods, such as:

- pizza slices
- pasta, potato or rice salad in a small tub
- a meat or vegetarian sausage
- soup in a flask
- tortilla wraps with interesting fillings
- slices of rolled up lean meat
- cheese dips or pâté with vegetable sticks
- a spring roll or samosa
- a chicken drumstick or wing.

Ways to a healthier lunch box

- Plan ahead. Make a plan of what you will pack in your children's lunch box for the week – this way, they'll stand a better chance of getting a balanced varied diet, and you won't need to go to the shops so often.

THE PERFECT LUNCH BOX

Lunch should supply about one-third of the daily energy requirements, as well as a third of protein, carbohydrate, fibre, vitamin and mineral needs.
Try to include:

- a 200–300 ml drink of water or fruit juice
- one portion of fresh or dried fruit
- one portion of salad or vegetables such as carrot sticks, cucumber or salad in a sandwich
- one carbohydrate food, such as bread, a roll or pasta salad
- one dairy food or calcium-rich food, such as cheese, yoghurt, fromage frais or milk
- one protein-rich food, such as meat, fish, peanut butter, hummus or egg.

Pack in an insulated lunch box with an ice pack to keep the meal fresh.

- Turn teatime leftovers into lunchbox ingredients for the next day:
    - Cold pasta, rice or potato can be made into a healthy salad and popped in a small tub.
    - Cold pizza slices can be wrapped in foil.
    - Home-made hot soup can be taken in a vacuum flask.
    - Cooked chicken drumsticks can be wrapped in foil.
- If your children like cereal bars, opt for those made with oats, nuts (check whether your school has a nut-free policy) and dried fruits. Avoid bars that list hydrogenated or vegetable fat or oil among the ingredients, or those that include several types of sugars (e.g. glucose syrup, invert sugar, fructose, sucrose) near the top of the ingredients list.

- Fruit bars are not a substitute for fresh fruit. Most are highly processed, contain high levels of concentrated sugars and stick very easily to the teeth.
- Keep hot foods hot in a vacuum container and cold foods cold. Include an ice pack with yoghurt, meat or any other foods that need chilling.
- Avoid the all-in-one lunch boxes targeted at young children. Most contain high levels of saturated fat and salt and don't provide much fibre or vitamins.
- Instead of crisps and other bagged snacks, try nuts (such as cashews, peanuts, almonds and brazils), seeds, plain popcorn, breadsticks and dried fruit. Handy small packs, including nut/seed/fruit mixes are now widely available from supermarkets.
- It's worth buying some small tubs that will fit easily into your children's box or bag. They are handy for packing ingredients such as pasta salad, dips, chopped fruit (such as apple, pineapple or kiwi slices), grapes, soft fruit (such as strawberries), dried fruit, nuts, vegetable sticks and cheese cubes.

Drinks

Lunchtime goal: between 200 and 300 ml each day

A lunchtime drink is important to keep children properly hydrated and avoid flagging energy levels in the afternoon. Even mild dehydration results in headaches, fatigue and poor concentration. Remember, children need six to eight glasses a day. Drinking plenty of fluid is also important to help their kidneys, brain and digestive system work properly.

Fruit and vegetables

Lunchtime goal: 1 portion of fruit and 1 portion of vegetables or salad

- Fruit and vegetables are much more appealing if they're quick and easy to eat. Give small fruit (e.g. little apples or satsumas, grapes or strawberries) or cut bigger fruits into bite-sized pieces.

- Small ring-pull tins of fruit in juice and small cartons of fruit purée – from supermarkets – are also tasty.

- Small boxes and bags of dried fruit are nutritious and fun to eat. My daughters adore dried tropical fruit and apricots (rich in beta-carotene and iron). But dried fruit can stick to the teeth, so encourage your children to follow with an apple and/or a piece of cheese (this reduces the acidity and helps re-mineralise the tooth enamel).

- Try fruit smoothies – they make a good alternative to whole fruit.

- Wrap carrot, pepper, cherry tomatoes, celery sticks or cucumber sticks in cling film or put in a small plastic pot. Serve with a small pot of hummus, salad cream or a cheesy dip. Add salad vegetables (e.g. salad leaves, tomatoes or cucumber) to sandwiches.

LESS SUITABLE DRINKS

- Fizzy drinks (contain too much sugar and too many artificial additives)

- Fruit drinks, squash and soft drinks (contain too much sugar and too many artificial additives)

BEST CHOICES

- Water

- Milk or milkshake (keep chilled in a thermos) (see recipes pages 155–157)

- Fruit juice (ideally diluted at least one part juice to one part water)

- Fruit smoothie (see recipes pages 155–157)

- Yoghurt drink (ideally probiotic varieties)

- Organic fruit cordial (diluted one part cordial to ten parts water)

MINI CHEESE AND VEGETABLE TARTLETTES

- ½ pack (200 g) ready-rolled shortcrust pastry
- 60 g (2 oz) Cheddar cheese
- 3 eggs
- 125 ml (4 fl oz) milk
- 2 tbsp sweetcorn
- 2 tbsp chopped red peppers
- 1 tomato, chopped

1 Pre-heat the oven to 200 °C/400 °F/Gas mark 6.
2 Butter or oil 6 holes of a deep muffin tin.
3 Place the ready-rolled pastry on a floured surface and cut into 6 rounds using an 8 cm (3") cutter.
4 Lightly press into the 6 muffin holes.
5 Combine the cheese, eggs and milk, and stir in the sweetcorn, peppers and tomato, then spoon into the muffin tin.
6 Bake in the oven for 20 minutes or until risen and golden.
7 Leave to cool for a few minutes before removing from the tin.

Sandwiches

Vary the type of bread you use for sandwiches. Try mini pittas, wraps (fill them then cut into lengths that small hands can cope with), bagels, small rolls or English muffins.

Use wholemeal or brown bread most of the time – it contains three times as much fibre and more iron and B vitamins. White bread with added fibre contains only a little more fibre than ordinary white.

Try using different types of bread – walnut bread, raisin or fruit bread, seeded bread or cheese and herb bread.

Sandwich fillings

Ideally, fillings should include a protein-rich food – cheese, chicken, ham, turkey, peanut butter, tuna or hummus – and a salad vegetable (e.g. cucumber or tomato).

BEST VEGETABLE CHOICES

- Sticks of carrots, cucumber, peppers
- Baby sweetcorn
- Tomato, cucumber, lettuce or cress in a sandwich filling
- Cherry tomatoes

BEST FRUIT CHOICES

- Apples, pears
- Satsumas, clementines, mandarins
- Bananas, grapes, cherries
- Kiwi fruit (children can cut them in half and scoop out the flesh with a spoon)
- Small container of strawberries, blueberries or raspberries
- Peaches, nectarines
- Small boxes of raisins
- Small bags of apricots, mango, pineapple, raisin or dried fruit
- Ring-pull cans or long-life cartons of fruit in juice
- Cartons and pots of fruit purée

Avoid sugary fillings such as jam or chocolate spread – they provide extra calories (in the form of sugar) but very few essential nutrients. Keep for occasional treats.

Stuck for ideas? Try the following nutritious fillings:

- Ham and tomato – lay three or four thin slices of tomato over a slice of lean ham.

- Peanut butter with cucumber – spread each slice of bread with peanut butter instead of your usual spread then lay several cucumber slices on top.

- Marmite and cheese – spread one slice of bread with Marmite (yeast extract) and cover with grated cheese.

- Soft cheese with tuna and lettuce – mix one tablespoon of soft cheese with an equal amount of tuna. Add shredded lettuce.

- Mozzarella and tomato – lay thin slices of mozzarella on one side of the bread and cover with thin tomato slices.

- Hardboiled egg mixed with mayonnaise and cress – mash one hard-boiled egg roughly with 2 teaspoons of mayonnaise. Stir in a little cress.

- Banana and honey – roughly mash half a banana with one teaspoon of lemon juice (to stop discolouration) and half a teaspoon of honey.

- Turkey slices with cranberry sauce – chop one or two slices of roast turkey with a teaspoon of cranberry sauce.

- Avocado and chicken – mash half an avocado with one teaspoon of lemon juice (to stop discolouration). Chop two slices of roast chicken and mix with the avocado.

- Hummus and grated carrot – mix one tablespoon of hummus (ready-made or see recipe on page 85) with one finely grated carrot.

- Cottage cheese and fruit – mix cottage cheese with raisins, chopped dried apricots or dried mango.

- Salmon and cucumber – roughly mash one tablespoon of tinned salmon and lay on top of thinly sliced cucumber.

- Chopped chicken and coleslaw – chop two slices of roast chicken and mix with one tablespoon of coleslaw.

- Banana and peanut butter.

- Sardine and cucumber.

- Chicken, tomato and mayonnaise.

- Cheese and peanut butter.

- Chicken, tomato and mayonnaise.

- Hummus (ready-made or see recipe on the next page) and cucumber.

Wraps

Soft flour wraps can be found in most supermarkets and make perfect wrappings for savoury fillings. Place the filling to the side of the centre of the wrap, fold over the unfilled half then roll up. Cut into 2 to 4 pieces to serve. For a lunch box, wrap in non-stick baking paper.

Try these yummy flavours:

- Cheese with tomato – mix 2 tablespoons of grated cheese with one chopped tomato.

- Egg and cress – roughly chop a hard-boiled or scrambled egg with one tablespoon of salad cream and a little cress.

- Chicken and lettuce – chop 2 cooked chicken slices and mix with 2 teaspoons of mayonnaise and some chopped lettuce.

- Tuna and cucumber – mix 2 tablespoons of tinned tuna with 2 teaspoons of mayonnaise and chopped cucumber.

- Cheese and carrots – mix equal amounts of grated cheddar cheese and grated carrots with a little salad cream (optional).

- Ham, tomato and cucumber – lay 2 slices of lean ham on the wrap and cover with slices of tomatoes and cucumber.

- Banana – toss one sliced banana in 1 teaspoon of lemon juice.

BREAD AND OTHER STARCHY FOODS

- Wholemeal, malted grain or wheatgerm bread
- Wholemeal roll
- Mini-pitta bread
- English muffin
- Mini-bagel
- Wrap
- Wholemeal crackers
- Rice cakes
- Pot of potato salad
- Pot of pasta or rice salad
- Slice of pizza

Calcium-rich foods

Lunch box goal: one dairy or soya serving

- Good dairy foods for lunches include cheese, yoghurt, fromage frais, milk or milkshake; or try a soya alternative – soya milk, soya 'yoghurt' or dessert. They all provide calcium, which is important for building healthy bones. Sardines and nuts (especially almonds) are another source of calcium.

- Try to buy yoghurt and fromage frais that doesn't contain artificial sweeteners, colours and flavourings. In general, organic varieties are best as they don't contain additives.

- Yoghurt pouches and tubes of fromage frais are great for eating on the go.

HUMMUS

This dip is an excellent source of fibre, protein and iron. Use as a filling for sandwiches or for dipping raw vegetables, such as carrot, pepper and cucumber sticks.

MAKES 4 SERVINGS

- *400 g (14 oz) tinned chickpeas*
- *2 garlic cloves, crushed*
- *2 tbsp (30 ml) extra virgin olive oil*
- *120 ml (4 fl oz) tahini (sesame seed paste)*
- *Juice of 1 lemon*
- *2–4 tbsp (30–60 ml) water*
- *A little low-sodium salt and freshly ground black pepper*
- *Pinch of paprika or cayenne pepper*

1 *Drain and rinse the chickpeas. Put them in a food processor or blender with the remaining ingredients, apart from the paprika. Process to a smooth paste. Add extra water if necessary to give the desired consistency.*
2 *Adjust the seasoning to taste.*
3 *Spoon into a serving dish. Pour over a little olive oil and sprinkle with cayenne or paprika.*
4 *Chill in the fridge for at least 2 hours before serving.*

PROTEIN-RICH AND CALCIUM-RICH FOODS FOR LUNCH BOXES

- Cheese in a sandwich
- Individual cheese portion
- Chicken drumsticks
- Low-fat sausages/vegetarian sausages
- Carton, pouch or tube of yoghurt*
- Carton, pouch or tube of fromage frais
- Carton or bottle of milk*
- Milkshake*
- Yoghurt drink*
- Carton of custard
- Pilchards in a sandwich
- Nuts (could be mixed with dried fruit or in a salad)

* Dairy or soya equivalent

Dips and snack pots

A tasty dip to dunk sticks of raw veg or breadsticks in can be part of a healthy lunch box for children.

For dipping

Carrot sticks, strips of cucumber and red peppers, baby sweetcorn or celery sticks.

Dips

Hummus (see recipe on page 85)
Avocado dip
Cheese dip
Cream cheese dips: mix together some cream cheese and natural/fruit yoghurt for dipping apple slices or grapes in

Snack pots

Fill small pots (you can use empty yoghurt pots) with any of the following:

- raisins, sultanas, pieces of dried apricot or other dried fruit

- grapes and satsuma segments

- home-made popcorn.

FRUIT MUFFINS

These are made with wholemeal flour; it contains fibre, iron and vitamins. Raisins also provide valuable fibre as well as lots of antioxidants.

MAKES 12 MUFFINS

- 125 g (4 oz) white self-raising flour
- 125 g (4 oz) wholemeal self-raising flour
- Pinch of salt
- 40 g (1½ oz) soft brown sugar
- 2 tbsp (30 ml) rapeseed oil
- 1 size 3 egg
- 200 ml (7 fl oz) milk
- 85 g (3 oz) raisins or sultanas

1 Pre-heat the oven to 220 °C/425 °F/Gas mark 7.
2 Mix the flours and salt together in a bowl.
3 Add the sugar, oil, egg and milk. Mix well.
4 Stir in the dried fruit.
5 Spoon into non-stick muffin tins and bake for 15–20 minutes until golden brown.

Extras

- Little extras make a varied lunch – try to provide healthy items most of the time (see box below).

- Chocolate-coated bars, cakes, crisps and biscuits shouldn't be included every day – they're loaded with unhealthy fats and sugar and are especially harmful to teeth if they're the last thing to be eaten.

- If children must have sugary foods, encourage them to eat a piece of fruit and a small piece of cheese afterwards – this helps counteract some of the damaging effects of sugar.

HEALTHIER EXTRAS

- Small packet of dried fruit (e.g. raisins, mango, apricots, dates, pineapple)
- A few nuts
- A few grapes
- Scone
- Fruit bun or teacake
- Mini-pancake
- Cereal bar (without hydrogenated fat)
- Breadsticks
- Rice cakes
- Plain popcorn
- Crisps that come with a separate packet of salt – remove the salt or add only half
- Home-made muffins, biscuits and fruit loaves (see recipes on pages 87–8 and 90–1)
- Small bags of dried fruit

BANANA LOAF

This healthy version of banana cake is made with wholemeal flour, brown sugar and rapeseed oil instead of the usual white flour, white sugar and butter.

MAKES 12 SLICES

- 225 g (8 oz) self-raising wholemeal flour
- 125 g (4 oz) brown sugar
- Pinch of salt
- ½ tsp each of mixed spice and cinnamon
- 2 large ripe bananas
- 175 ml (6 fl oz) orange juice
- 2 size 3 eggs
- 4 tbsp (60 ml) rapeseed oil

1 Pre-heat the oven to 170 °C/325 °F/Gas mark 4.
2 Mix together the flour, sugar, salt and spices in a bowl.
3 Mash the bananas with the orange juice.
4 Combine the mashed banana mixture, eggs and oil with the flour mixture.
5 Spoon into a lightly oiled 2 lb loaf tin.
6 Bake for about 1 hour. Check the cake is done by inserting a skewer or knife into the centre. It should come out clean.

BANANA MUFFINS

These tasty banana muffins are made with healthy rapeseed oil, which is rich in essential fats (including omega-3 fats).

MAKES 12 MUFFINS

- 2 large ripe bananas, mashed
- 85 g (3 oz) soft brown sugar
- 4 tbsp (60 ml) rapeseed oil
- 1 size 3 egg
- 125 ml (4 fl oz) milk
- 200 g (7 oz) self-raising flour
- Pinch of salt
- ½ tsp (2.5 ml) nutmeg, grated

1 Preheat the oven to 190 °C/375 °F/Gas mark 5.
2 In a bowl, mix together the bananas, sugar and oil.
3 Beat in the egg and milk.
4 Fold in the flour, salt and nutmeg.
5 Spoon into non-stick muffin tins and bake for 15–20 minutes.

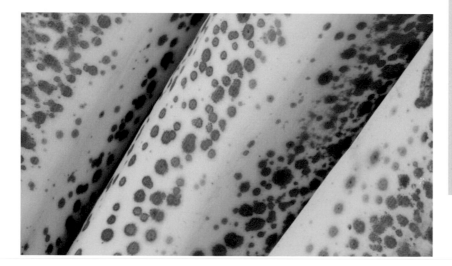

APRICOT BARS

Dried apricots are packed with beta-carotene, a powerful antioxidant that boosts immunity and protects against illness.

MAKES 8 BARS

- 125 g (4 oz) self-raising white flour
- 60 g (2 oz) sugar
- 125 g (4 oz) dried apricots
- 6 tbsp (90 ml) orange juice
- 2 size 3 eggs
- 125 g (4 oz) sultanas

1 Preheat the oven to 180 °C/350 °F/Gas mark 4.
2 Mix together the flour and sugar in a bowl.
3 Blend together the apricots and juice in a liquidiser until smooth.
4 Add the apricot purée, eggs and sultanas to the flour and sugar. Mix.
5 Spoon the mixture into an 18 cm (7 in) square cake tin. Bake for 30–35 minutes until golden brown. Allow to cool. Cut into 8 bars.

DELICIOUSLY CLEVER: ONE MONTH OF LUNCHBOXES				
	WEEK 1	**WEEK 2**	**WEEK 3**	**WEEK 4**
Monday	Wholemeal chicken and tomato sandwich 1 pot of fruit yoghurt 6–7 carrot sticks 1 satsuma Apple juice (diluted 50/50 with water).	Mini-bagel filled with soft cheese and sliced banana 1 small bunch of grapes 1 pot of fromage frais Bottle of water	Wholemeal roll with tuna, sweetcorn and mayonnaise 6–7 carrot sticks Individual cheese portion Small bag of dried fruit (e.g. mango, pineapple) Bottle of water	Rice salad with cooked chicken, peas and sweetcorn 1 pear Milkshake
Tuesday	Flask of vegetable soup Wholemeal roll and butter Small bag of dried fruit Individual cheese portion Orange juice (diluted 50/50 with water)	Mini tartlette (see recipe page 82) 6–7 carrot sticks 1 pot of fromage frais Fruit smoothie	4 wholemeal crackers Hummus dip Vegetable sticks, e.g. cucumber, carrots, celery Handful of grapes 1 pot of fruit yoghurt Bottle of water	Flask of tomato soup 1 wholemeal cheese roll 1 satsuma 1 wholemeal raisin biscuit (see recipe page 90) Bottle of water
Wednesday	Slice of homemade pizza 4–5 strips of peppers or 4–5 cherry tomatoes 1 apple 1 yoghurt drink	Cooked tofu sausage or quorn sausage (wrapped in foil) Wholemeal Marmite sandwich Small handful of nuts in a pot (e.g. cashews, peanuts) 1 clementine Bottle of water	1 cooked chicken drumstick (wrapped in foil) Small Marmite sandwich 1 plum Apple juice (ideally, diluted 50/50 with water)	Cheese dip or pâté Carrot, pepper and cucumber sticks A few breadsticks 1 pear Yoghurt drink
Thursday	Pasta salad with tuna, peppers and mushrooms 1 pot of fruit yoghurt 1 small bag of dried apricots Apple juice (diluted 50/50 with water)	Mini wholemeal pitta filled with tinned salmon and salad Handful of cherries Mini box of raisins Yoghurt drink	1 bagel of soft cheese and sliced cucumber 4 cherry tomatoes 1 ring-pull can of fruit in juice Bottle of water	Wholemeal roll filled with chicken and coleslaw Cereal bar (see recipe page 91) 1 apple Milkshake
Friday	Tortilla wrap filled with cooked turkey and coleslaw 1 small ring-pull tin of fruit in juice 1 carton of milk	Mixed bean salad (in a tub) 1 peach 1 carton of custard Orange juice (diluted 50/50 with water)	Wrap filled with ham, tomato and cucumber slices 1 banana Yoghurt drink	Wholemeal peanut butter and cucumber roll Individual cheese portion Strawberries (in a tub) 1 pot of fromage frais Bottle of water

WHOLEMEAL RAISIN BISCUITS

These biscuits are far healthier than bought ones. They're lower in sugar and higher in fibre.

MAKES 20 BISCUITS

- *225 g (8 oz) wholemeal plain flour*
- *40 g (1½ oz) brown sugar*
- *85 g (3 oz) raisins*
- *2 tbsp (30 ml) rapeseed oil*
- *1 size 3 egg*
- *4 tbsp (60 ml) milk*

1 *Pre-heat the oven to 180°C/350°F/Gas mark 4.*
2 *Combine the flour, sugar and raisins in a bowl.*
3 *Stir in the oil, egg and milk and lightly mix to a stiff dough.*
4 *Place spoonfuls of the mixture on to a lightly oiled baking tray.*
5 *Bake for 12–15 minutes until golden brown.*

Q&A

Question: What should I do when my daughter asks for crisps and biscuits in her lunch box so she can eat the same things as her friends?

Answer: No child likes to be different. But you don't have to surrender your principles. You can compromise by allowing crisps – ideally the lower salt kind – one day of the week.

As for other favourite snacks, why not make your own biscuits (see Wholemeal raisin biscuits, opposite) or muffins (see Fruit muffins, page 86)? When my eldest daughter first took a kiwi fruit with a small knife and spoon to school, her friends were so intrigued they requested one too! Let your child choose her own healthy treats – small bags of dried fruit, small ring-pull tins of fruit, novelty cheeses or yoghurt tubes.

Summary

- Make sure the lunch box you provide is attractive, varied and imaginative.

- Keep it balanced; include a drink, a portion of fresh or dried fruit, a portion of salad or vegetables, some carbohydrate (wholemeal bread, pasta or rice), a dairy or calcium-rich food, and a protein-rich food (meat, cheese, peanut butter).

- Vary the type of bread you use for sandwiches – try seeded bread, mini pittas, tortilla wraps, bagels or fancy rolls.

- Instead of sandwiches every day, try pizza slices, pasta, potato or rice salad, a sausage, soup in a flask, slices of rolled up lean meat, dips or pâté with vegetable sticks, or a chicken drumstick.

- Give fruit in a form that can be easily eaten – small fruits, easy-to-peel varieties or fruit cut into bite-sized pieces.

- The easiest way to include vegetables in a lunch box is to cut them into manageable pieces (e.g. carrot sticks), add them to a sandwich filling or mix them with pasta in a salad.

- Instead of sugary foods and crisps, try small packets of dried fruit, a few nuts, grapes, a scone or fruit bun, plain popcorn, or healthier home-made muffins, biscuits and fruit loaves.

- If children occasionally have sugary foods, encourage them to follow with a piece of fruit and a small piece of cheese – this helps counteract some of the damaging effects of sugar.

CEREAL BARS

These highly nutritious bars are made from oats and muesli, which provide lots of fibre, B vitamins and sustained energy. They're lower in fat than shop-bought cereal bars.

MAKES 12 BARS

- 175 g (6 oz) oats
- 85 g (3 oz) no added sugar
- muesli
- 150 g (5 oz) dried fruit mixture
- 3 tbsp (45 ml) honey, clear or set
- 2 egg whites
- 175 ml (6 fl oz) apple juice

1 Pre-heat the oven to 180°C/ 350°F/Gas mark 4.
2 Combine the oats, muesli and dried fruit in a bowl.
3 Warm the honey in a small saucepan until it is runny. Add to the bowl.
4 Stir in the remaining ingredients.
5 Press the mixture into a lightly oiled 18 × 28 cm (7 × 11 in) baking tin. Bake for 20–25 minutes until golden.
6 When cool, cut into bars.

8 active kids

Healthy eating is only one part of a healthy lifestyle. Activity, like a good diet, needs to be part of children's lives too. It'll help keep children slim, fit and full of energy.

Exercise is good for boosting children's self-esteem and mental well-being, and teaches them numerous extra skills such as balance, coordination and concentration. Being more competent at basic physical skills increases their confidence and helps them feel more positive about themselves. Surveys by the Qualifications and Curriculum Agency have shown that sporty pupils achieve higher grades and are better behaved at school.

However, a Health Survey for England found that one-third of boys and girls aged 2–11 years don't get the minimum exercise they need (60 minutes of physical activity a day). P.E. lesson cutbacks, loss of school and community playing fields, too much watching television and playing on computers are blamed – as is being driven to school.

Benefits of activity

There are many reasons to exercise, even if kids aren't too keen to get going at first:

- Exercise benefits the heart – energetic activities such as running and swimming get the heart pumping and stronger at delivering oxygen around the body.

- Exercise develops stronger muscles – anything from climbing frames to ball games works.

- Exercise increases flexibility – encourage children to try gymnastics, dancing and martial arts to keep them supple.

- Exercise boosts mood – it helps the body release 'feel-good' chemicals called endorphins, reduces stress and anxiety and makes children feel good about themselves.

GETTING TO SCHOOL

Seven in ten children are driven to school despite living less than a mile away, according to a 2006 survey of 5–12-year-old children. Fewer than 1 per cent of children cycle to school and more than 80 per cent watch more than one hour of television each day during the school week.

- Exercise keeps children slim – any activity burns calories, reducing the risk of children becoming overweight. It also helps appetite control so they naturally won't overeat.

- Exercise can make them smarter – it improves kids' concentration, creativity and reasoning.

Upping the action

Make plenty of opportunities for children to be active and to build activity into the family's daily routine. Your kids' days should be as action-packed as possible. Walking to and from school and other nearby places, riding a bike to visit friends and playing active games will help them see exercise as a way of life.

Ways to build activity into children's lives include:

- Walk or cycle to school with your kids.

- Increase the whole family's exercise by enjoying activities together – swimming, playing football, frisbee, tennis, a family bike ride or walk.

- Lead by example – show your child that you value activity by taking part yourself.

- Keep it fun – it is vital that children have fun with any activities they do. If they are enthusiastic about activity or sport they'll stick to it.

- Add purpose to activities – walking the dog, joining a swimming club or entering family charity sports events.

- Get them helping with household chores (such as vacuuming and washing the car) and gardening.

- Provide plenty of play equipment at home.

- Encourage them to enjoy a wide range of sports.

- Give your child a chance to practise skills such as running, jumping, throwing, catching and kicking – either with you or with friends.

- Find fun, active ways to celebrate special occasions – a hike and a picnic, or a disco birthday party.

P.E. AT SCHOOL

The government recommends children do at least 2 hours of P.E. and sport at school each week. However, a 2004 survey by the Department for Education and Skills found that only one in three 5- and 6-year-olds, and half of primary pupils, meet the target. On average, primary-school children spend 92 to 100 minutes on sport each week, one of the lowest rates in Europe.

- Encourage them to join active clubs at school, for example football, netball or tennis, or after-school activity sports clubs at the leisure centre, local community centre or local sports club.

- Make sport sociable – children are more likely to participate if their friends are involved too. Take a group to the swimming pool or ice rink.

Five top activity tips

1 Give them plenty of support and encouragement – but don't allow your children's sport to become your obsession.

2 It is important that children learn a good range of movement skills – running, throwing, catching – and not just skills that are specific to one sport.

3 The focus, especially with the under 12s, should be on enjoyment.

4 Children under 12 years should do a range of sports and not begin to specialise until they are at least 11 years old.

5 If training for a sport is started too early, children can burn out either physically (through injury or fatigue) or mentally (through boredom or stress) by their teens.

SAFETY MEASURES

Always take precautions to ensure your child's safety when being active. Make sure they wear any necessary protective equipment, e.g. a cycle helmet, check the area in which they are playing is safe, and ensure they have adequate supervision (this is important but, if possible, do try and let your child practice some independence).

How much exercise?

2–5-year-olds: Play games with them every day. Aim for short bursts of activity that develop basic skills such as running, jumping and coordination. Try:

- Playing catch
- Skipping
- Tag
- Swimming
- Riding a bike
- Frisbee
- Hopscotch

6–10-year-olds: 60 minutes of moderate intensity activity as part of their lifestyle every day. It doesn't have to be done in one go – it can be built up over the day through, for example, four 15-minute periods of activity, three 20-minute periods or two 30-minutes periods. This could include walking to and from school, P.E. lessons, active play with friends at break times and out of school, sport or structured exercise. Try:

- Tennis
- Dancing
- In-line skating
- Active play such as ball games, chase and hide and seek
- Swimming
- Riding a bike
- Most sports and P.E., e.g. football, netball
- Playground games

It is also recommended that at least twice a week, some activities should help to enhance strength and flexibility and bone health. This could include:

- Climbing
- Skipping
- Ballet
- Gymnastics
- Martial arts

11–15-year-olds: 30–60 minutes of moderate to vigorous activity every day as part of their lifestyle. Plus three sessions per week of continuous vigorous activity lasting at least 20 minutes. This could include

- Running/ jogging
- Athletics
- In-line skating
- Tennis or badminton
- Swimming
- Cycling
- Dancing or aerobic classes
- Team sports, e.g. rugby, football, hockey and netball

Should children do strength training?

Sports scientists say that children over 10 years can include strength training in their overall training programme, provided it is properly designed and supervised The American College of Sports Medicine and American Academy of Paediatrics Committee on Sports Medicine recommends the following guidelines:

- Children should be properly supervised during training sessions.
- They should use an age-appropriate routine (adult routines are not suitable).
- Ensure the exercises are performed using proper form and technique.
- Children should start with a relatively light weight and a high number of repetitions.

■ No heavy lifts should be included. Avoid power lifting and bodybuilding.

■ The programme should form part of a total fitness programme.

■ The sessions should be varied and fun.

CALORIE CLASS

Below is the estimated calorie burn for activities when they are performed by a 10-year old who weighs 33kg (about 5 stone). Heavier children will burn slightly more calories, and lighter children will burn less.

Activity	Calories in 30 minutes
Cycling (11.2 km/h)	88
Running (12 km/h)	248
Sitting	24
Standing	26
Swimming (crawl, 4.8 km/h)	353
Tennis	125
Walking	88

Values are based on measurements made on adults, scaled down to the body weight of 33 kg, with an added margin of 25 per cent. Heavier children will burn slightly more calories; lighter children will burn less.

Fuelling active kids

Kids need fuel for exercise so feed them a healthy diet to keep their energy levels up.

Energy

The biggest nutritional difference between active children and their less active friends is the amount of energy (calories) they need to consume. The more active they are and the more they weigh, the more calories they need. For example, a girl who weighs 40 kg and spends 1–2 hours daily training/ playing sport would need 2201 Calories a day. That's more than the average (non-active) adult woman who (according to government guidelines) needs only

---

SHOULD KIDS EXERCISE HARD OR GENTLY?

More intense workouts may be better at keeping kids slim. A 2006 Swedish study published in the American Journal of Clinical Nutrition found that 9- and 10-year-old children who did at least 40 minutes vigorous activity (e.g. cycling, swimming) had less body fat than those who did less than 20 minutes daily.

2000 calories, and certainly more than a typical (non-active) 10-year-old who needs 1740 calories daily.

Of course, I'm not suggesting you should be counting your kids' calories – far from it – but you need to be aware how much they need to eat. In this case, the 10-year-old needs to eat 26 per cent more than her classmates.

Be guided, too, by your child's energy levels. If they are persistently tired and lethargic when it comes to training (despite getting enough sleep) they may not be eating enough. If they appear to have plenty of energy and get-up-and-go, then they are probably eating enough.

ESTIMATED AVERAGE REQUIREMENTS FOR ENERGY OF CHILDREN*		
AGE	BOYS (KCAL)	GIRLS (KCAL)
4–6 years	1715	1545
7–10 years	1970	1740
11–14 years	2220	1845
15–18 years	2755	2110

* Dept of Health Dietary Reference Values for food energy and nutrients for the United Kingdom (1991) London: HMSO

Protein

Active children should be able to get enough protein by eating two to four portions of protein-rich foods daily as well as balanced amounts of grains and dairy foods, all of which also supply smaller amounts of protein.

Vegetarian children need to ensure they eat a wide variety of plant proteins: beans, lentils, grains, nuts, seeds, soya and quorn.

Eating before training

Food eaten before exercise needs to stop children feeling hungry during training, be easily digested and have a moderate to low GI. The exact timing will probably

depend on practical constraints: for example the training session may be straight after school, leaving very little time to eat.

If there is less than one hour between eating and training, give them a light snack (see 'Pre-exercise snacks' right). If they have more than two hours between eating and training, their normal balanced meal will be suitable. This should be based around a carbohydrate food such as bread or potatoes together with a little protein such as chicken or beans, as well as a portion of vegetables and a drink (see 'Pre-exercise meals' right).

Try to steer children away from sugary foods such as sweets and soft drinks just before exercising. This may cause a quick surge of blood glucose and insulin followed by a rapid fall, which may result in hypoglycaemia (low blood sugar levels) and early fatigue.

Drinking before training

Make sure children are well hydrated before exercise. If they are slightly dehydrated at this stage there is a bigger risk of overheating once they start exercising. Encourage them to drink 6–8 cups (1–1.5 litres) of fluid during the day and, as a final measure, top up with 150–200 ml (a large glass) of water 45 minutes before exercise.

Eating during training

If children will be exercising continually for less than 90 minutes, they won't need to eat anything during exercise. They should, however, be encouraged to take regular drink breaks, ideally every 15–20 minutes or whenever there is a suitable break in training. Make sure they take a water bottle and keep it within easy reach, for example by the track, pool or pitch.

Thirst things first

Children can easily forget to drink during training, becoming oblivious to thirst as they focus on beating their friends or just having fun.

The most important thing is that children drink enough and don't become dehydrated. Therefore, the taste is important. If they don't like it, they won't drink it! Many children are not very keen on drinking water so they may not drink enough. Water tends to quench one's thirst even if the body is still dehydrated.

PRE-EXERCISE SNACKS

(Eaten approximately 1 hour before exercise with a drink of water)

Fresh fruit and glass of milk

Small peanut butter sandwich

Cereal bar or dried fruit bar

Pot of fruit yoghurt and a banana or apple

Small packet of dried fruit, e.g. apricots, raisins

Breakfast cereal with milk

Yoghurt drink

Flavoured milk

Wholemeal crackers or rice cakes with a little cheese

PRE-EXERCISE MEALS

(Eaten 2–3 hours before exercise with a drink of water)

Sandwich/roll/bagel/wrap filled with tuna, cheese, chicken or peanut butter

Jacket potato with cheese, tuna or baked beans

Pasta with tomato-based sauce

Rice or noodles with chicken or lentils

Breakfast cereal with milk and banana

Porridge with raisins

Lentil, vegetable or chicken soup with wholemeal bread

Diluted pure fruit juice, sugar-free squash or ordinary diluted squash are acceptable alternatives to water. (Organic squashes are better options, although they are more expensive.)

Sports drinks or energy drinks are not necessary for activities lasting less than 90 minutes (compared with water or flavoured drinks), but if children prefer the taste they may be encouraged to drink larger volumes of fluid. But a word of caution: in practice, many children find that sports drinks sit 'heavily' in their stomachs. So, you may either dilute the sports drink with water (if making up from powder, add a little extra water) or alternate sports drinks with water.

After training

After training, the number one priority is to replenish fluid losses. So give children a drink straight away – water or diluted fruit juice are the best drinks.

They also need to replace the energy they have just used. Unless they will be eating a meal within half an hour, give them a snack to stave off hunger and promote recovery.

WHY CHILDREN ARE MORE AT RISK OF DEHYDRATION:

- They sweat less than adults (sweat helps keep the body's temperature stable).

- They cannot cope with very hot conditions as well as adults can.

- They get hotter during exercise.

- They have a greater surface area for their body weight.

- They often fail to recognise or respond to feelings of thirst.

HOW TO GET CHILDREN TO DRINK ENOUGH

- Make drinking more fun with a novelty water bottle.

- Make sure they place the bottle within easy access, e.g. by the side of the track they pass most frequently.

- Ask the coach to schedule drink breaks – encourage them to take regular sips, ideally every 10–20 minutes. This may take practice.

- Tell them not to wait until they are thirsty.

- If they don't like water, offer a flavoured drink such as diluted fruit juice, diluted squash or a diluted sports drink.

- Chill the drink (to around 10 °C) or add some ice cubes; this usually encourages children to drink more.

Are junk foods really that bad for active kids?

Many parents turn a blind eye to their kids eating things such as crisps and sweets because 'they'll burn it off anyway'. The truth is that these foods are still displacing foods that provide important vitamins, minerals and fibre. A child filling up on sweets and crisps misses out on the nutrients they would otherwise get from, for example, a wholemeal cheese sandwich, a piece of fruit or a yoghurt.

Of course, active kids need more calories but they also need more vitamins (to convert the food into energy), minerals (for making more red blood cells) and protein (to repair muscles after training). Once they have met their daily targets for fruit and veg, grains, protein-rich and calcium-rich foods and healthy fats then it is fine to have one or two treats.

Try to get them to favour treats such as chocolate-covered nuts, low-fat frozen yogurt, ice cream, fruit cake, malt loaf, cereal bars (without hydrogenated oils), dark chocolate containing 70 per cent cocoa solids, fig rolls, milkshakes or rice pudding.

Q&A

Question: How can I persuade my junk food addict to eat more healthily?

Answer: Re-educating a junk food addict is difficult. You can control what your children eat at home – and the solution is to not to have junk foods in the house – but you cannot see what they eat at school or outside the house.

The best approach is to instil a positive attitude about healthy food choices. Link healthy food with something that matters to your children: better running, faster times, more energy. Don't ban any foods or convey an evangelical attitude to healthy eating. Children of any age are more likely to copy what you do than what you say. Share mealtimes as often as possible and eat the same foods.

If they insist on eating junk food, try to limit it to one junk food item a day. If they do have a junk food meal (outside the house), encourage them to add a salad, a serving of vegetables or a bowl of fresh fruit. Try to redress the balance by providing a healthier nutrient-packed meal at home.

SUITABLE RECOVERY SNACKS

(Accompany all snacks with a drink of water or diluted fruit juice)

Fruit cake or malt loaf
Fresh fruit, e.g. bananas, grapes and apples
Packet of dried fruit and nuts
Fruit yoghurt or yoghurt drink
Smoothie (bought or home-made)
Jam or honey sandwich or roll
Mini-pancakes
Chocolate-coated nuts and raisins
Flavoured milk

SUITABLE RECOVERY MEALS

(Accompany all meals with a drink of water or diluted fruit juice and 1–2 portions of vegetables or salad)

Jacket potato with beans, tuna or cheese
Pasta with tomato sauce and cheese
Rice with chicken and stir-fried vegetables
Fish pie
Baked beans on toast
Fish cakes or falafel with a jacket potato

JUNK FOOD SWAPS

Replace:	With:
Crisps/salty packet snacks	Plain popcorn Low-fat baked potato crisps Twiglets Mini rice cakes
Biscuits	Rice cakes with peanut butter or cheese A couple of fig rolls
Shop-bought cakes	Wholemeal hot cross bun/fruit bun Slice of malt loaf
Sweets	Packet of dried fruit, e.g. raisins, apricots, tropical fruits Packet of nuts Dried apple rings and a few nuts Pre-made fruit salads Fruit bags
Chocolate bar	Cereal/nut/fruit bar
Cola	Water Fruit juice (ideally diluted 50/50) Low-fat milk or flavoured milk Yoghurt drink Smoothie

9   fun with food

Kids in the kitchen

Cooking can be great fun for children. Creating their own dishes gives them a sense of achievement, and can be a superb way to motivate fussy eaters to try new tastes and gain confidence with food. Preparing meals can also be educational; children quickly pick up new skills when they're enjoying themselves – they'll learn about weighing, measuring, mixing, spreading, cutting, organising and following instructions, as well as finding out how ingredients work together.

Try these eight recipes; they're easy enough for older children to make on their own. (Younger children may need help from an adult.)

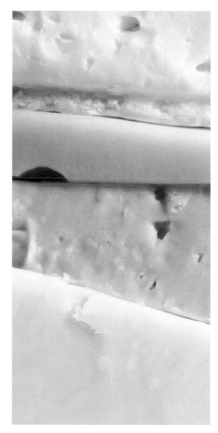

STRIPY CHEESE ON TOAST

MAKES 2 PORTIONS

- *2 slices of bread*
- *40 g (1½ oz) Cheddar cheese*
- *40 g (1½ oz) Red Leicester cheese*
- *You'll need: a sharp knife, chopping board, grill pan*

1 *Pre-heat the grill.*
2 *Toast the bread on both sides in a toaster or under the grill.*
3 *Slice the cheese into strips about 2 cm (¾ in) wide and 5 mm (¼ in) thick.*
4 *Lay alternating slices of Cheddar and Red Leicester on the toast until the toast is covered.*
5 *Place the toast on the grill rack and place under the grill for about one minute until the cheese has melted and started bubbling.*

BREADSTICKS

MAKES ABOUT 20

- *750 g (1½ lb) strong white flour*
- *7 g (1 sachet) easy blend yeast*
- *450 ml (¾ pint) warm water*
- *1 tsp salt*
- *1 tbsp olive oil*

You'll need: a large mixing bowl, a wooden spoon, a knife, 2 baking trays, clingfilm, oven gloves

1 *Put the flour, yeast, warm water, salt and olive oil into a mixing bowl.*
2 *Mix them together using a wooden spoon, then use your hands to bring the mixture together.*
3 *Sprinkle the worktop with flour and take the mixture out of the bowl. Knead the dough for 10 minutes. It should be smooth and stretchy, not sticky.*
4 *Cut the dough into about 20 pieces. Roll each out to make a 25 cm (10 inch) long stick.*
5 *Grease the baking trays. Put the breadsticks spaced apart on to the trays. Cover loosely with clingfilm and leave in a warm place until the breadsticks have doubled in size – about 30 minutes.*
6 *Meanwhile heat the oven to 200 °C/400 °F/Gas mark 6.*
7 *Remove the clingfilm and bake the breadsticks in the oven for 6–8 minutes until golden.*

tip *You can make different shapes with the bread dough or decorate with beaten egg and sunflower or poppy seeds just before putting in the oven.*

VEGETABLE SOUP

MAKES 4 SERVINGS

- 1 large onion
- 1 red pepper
- 2 large carrots
- 1 potato
- 1 tbsp olive oil
- 2 tsp Swiss vegetable bouillon powder or 1 vegetable stock cube
- 900 ml (1½ pints) water

You'll need: chopping board, vegetable peeler, sharp knife, large saucepan with a lid, wooden spoon

1 *On the chopping board, peel then chop the onion.*
2 *Cut the pepper in half, cut away the white pith and scrape away the seeds. Cut into small squares.*
3 *Using the vegetable peeler, peel and cut the carrots and potato into small pieces (you may need to ask an adult to help).*
4 *Put the oil in the saucepan and put over a low heat. Add the onions and cook for 5 minutes, stirring with a wooden spoon until see-through and soft.*
5 *Add the rest of the vegetables and stock powder/cube. Pour in the water. Bring the mixture to the boil, cover then turn down the heat and simmer for 30 minutes over a low heat.*
6 *The soup is ready to serve. If you don't like lumpy soup, use a blender until it's smooth. Let the soup cool before blending (you may need to ask an adult to help you use a blender).*

CHOCOLATE CHIP MUFFINS

MAKES 12

- 250 g (9 oz) self-raising flour
- 85 g (3 oz) sugar
- 200 ml (7 fl oz) milk
- 1 egg
- ½ tsp (2.5 ml) vanilla extract
- 85 g (3 oz) butter or margarine, melted
- 85 g (3 oz) chocolate chips

You'll need: a muffin tin, 12 paper cases, mixing bowl, wooden spoon, metal spoon

1 *Heat the oven to 200 °C/400 °F/Gas mark 6.*
2 *Line the muffin tin with paper cases.*
3 *Mix together the flour and sugar in a large bowl.*
4 *Combine the milk, egg, vanilla extract and melted butter or margarine in a separate bowl.*
5 *Pour the liquid ingredients into a well in the flour mixture. Mix together.*
6 *Add the chocolate chips and combine briefly.*
7 *Spoon the mixture into the muffin tin. Bake for about 15 minutes or until risen and golden.*

JACKET POTATO WITH TUNA AND CUCUMBER

- *4 potatoes*
- *200 g (7 oz) tin tuna*
- *Half a cucumber*
- *4 tbsp mayonnaise*

You'll need: vegetable brush, fork, tin opener, small bowl, chopping board, small sharp knife, metal spoon

1 *Heat the oven to 200°C/400°F/Gas mark 6.*
2 *Scrub the potatoes with the vegetable brush. Prick the skin with a fork. Bake in the oven for about 1 hour or until the flesh is soft.*
3 *Meanwhile, open the can of tuna and drain off the liquid. Put the tuna in a bowl and break it roughly with a fork.*
4 *On the chopping board, cut the cucumber in half lengthways. Cut each half in half lengthways again. Cut each segment into slices about 5 mm (¼ inch) thick.*
5 *Add the cucumber to the tuna with the mayonnaise. Mix together with the spoon.*
6 *Remove the potatoes from the oven (ask an adult to help with this). Cut a cross in the top of each potato and gently prise open (again, ask an adult to help). Spoon the tuna and cucumber mixture over the top of the potatoes.*

Here are some other toppings for jacket potatoes:

baked beans
grated cheddar cheese
crème fraiche
salsa
stir-fried vegetables
chopped chicken or turkey mixed
   with a little mayonnaise
hummus
cottage cheese
prawns with mayonnaise
ratatouille
grilled mushrooms
chilli (see recipe page 127)
scrambled egg and tomato
sweetcorn

SULTANA SCONES

MAKES 12

- *225 g (8 oz) self-raising flour*
- *60 g (2 oz) butter or margarine*
- *60 g (2 oz) caster sugar*
- *60 g (2 oz) sultanas*
- *150 ml (¼ pint) milk*

You'll need: mixing bowl, palette knife, baking sheet, rolling pin, 5 cm (2 in) cutter, oven gloves, wire rack

1 *Heat the oven to 230 °C/450 °F/Gas mark 8.*
2 *Grease a baking sheet with butter or margarine.*

3 *Put the flour in a mixing bowl. Add the margarine and rub in with your fingertips until the mixture looks like fine breadcrumbs. Stir in the sultanas.*
4 *Stir in enough milk to form a soft dough, using the palette knife.*
5 *Sprinkle flour on the work surface and knead the dough lightly for a few moments.*
6 *Roll out the dough until 2 cm (¾ inch) thick. Cut out rounds with a floured cutter and place on the greased baking sheet.*
7 *Bake in the oven for 10 minutes until risen and golden. Transfer to a wire rack to cool.*

FRUIT SMOOTHIE

You can use other varieties of fresh fruit or even frozen or tinned fruit. Try making a smoothie with mango and peach, or apple and banana. Just add fruit juice or milk and yoghurt. You may need to ask an adult to help you use the blender.

MAKES 2 GLASSES

- *6 strawberries*
- *1 handful of raspberries*
- *1 banana*
- *450 ml (¾ pint) milk or orange juice*
- *1 tbsp yoghurt*

You'll need: a knife, chopping board, smoothie maker, blender or food processor

1 *Slice the green tops off the strawberries. Peel the banana and cut into thick slices.*
2 *Put the fruit into the smoothie maker, blender or food processor.*
3 *Add the milk or orange juice and the yoghurt.*
4 *Put the lid on the machine and blend together for about 30 seconds.*
5 *Pour into two glasses.*

good health on a plate

Menu plans for balanced eating

Variety is the key to healthy, balanced eating, so aim to use the following menu plans as a basis for developing your child's daily diet. These menus are in line with the dietary recommendations of the children's food guide pyramid (*see* page 16) and provide a good balance of carbohydrate, protein, fat, vitamins and minerals.

There are two seven-day menu plans for 5–10-year-olds and two seven-day menu plans for 11–15-year-olds, each including a vegetarian eating plan. Judge the portion sizes according to your children's age, activity and appetite. Encourage your children to drink six to eight glasses of fluid (water, diluted fruit juice or milk) daily, and more during exercise or in hot weather.

SEVEN-DAY MENU PLAN FOR 5–10-YEAR-OLDS	
Monday	
Breakfast	Wholegrain cereal with milk
	Banana
Lunchbox	Tuna, cucumber and mayonnaise wholemeal sandwich
	Small ring-pull can of fruit in juice
	Carton of yoghurt
	Water
Dinner	Chicken burgers
	Oven potato wedges (*see* recipe page 137)
	Baked beans or broccoli
	Stewed apples and raisins

SEVEN-DAY MENU PLAN FOR 5–10-YEAR-OLDS (CONTINUED)

Tuesday	
Breakfast	Wholemeal toast and peanut butter or Marmite
	Fresh fruit
	Milk or yoghurt
Lunchbox	Slice of pizza
	Raw carrot and cucumber sticks
	Small bunch of seedless grapes
	Pot of fromage frais
	Orange juice
Dinner	Pasta and tuna bake
	Sliced tomatoes with a little dressing
	Yoghurt and fruit pudding
Wednesday	
Breakfast	Porridge made with milk and water
	A little honey and raisins
Lunchbox	Pitta bread filled with cold chopped chicken and coleslaw
	4–5 dried apricots
	Small carton of milk
Dinner	Toad-and-veggies-in-the-hole (*see* recipe page 125)
	Spring cabbage or broccoli
	Fresh fruit
Thursday	
Breakfast	Banana smoothie (*see* recipe page 155)
Lunchbox	Wholemeal roll filled with lean ham and tomato
	Piece of fresh fruit
	Carton of custard
	Water
Dinner	Jacket potato filled with baked beans and grated cheese or scrambled egg and tomato
	Crunchy apple crumble (*see* recipe page 146)

SEVEN-DAY MENU PLAN FOR 5–10-YEAR-OLDS (CONTINUED)

Friday

Breakfast	Bowl of fresh fruit, e.g. oranges, pineapple and mango
	1 pot of fruit yoghurt
Lunchbox	Cheese dip or hummus (*see* recipe page 149), breadsticks
	Raw vegetable sticks, e.g. carrot, pepper and cucumber
	Small box of raisins
	Milkshake
Supper	Chicken in tomato sauce (*see* recipe page 122)
	Boiled rice, peas
	Fresh fruit

Saturday

Breakfast	Boiled egg and wholemeal toast
	Orange juice
Lunch	Potato soup (*see* recipe page 139)
	Grated cheese
	Granary roll
	Fresh fruit salad
Supper	Home-made chicken nuggets (*see* recipe page 122)
	Mighty root mash (*see* recipe page 136)
	Carrots and peas
	Baked rice pudding (*see* recipe page 146)

Sunday

Breakfast	Pancakes filled with apple purée (*see* recipe page 145)
Lunch	Jacket potato
	Grilled chicken
	Broccoli and carrots
	Raspberry fool (*see* recipe page 24)
Supper	1 slice of homemade pizza (*see* recipe page 129)
	Salad, e.g. cherry tomatoes, peppers, grated carrot, cucumber
	A little salad dressing
	Fresh fruit

SEVEN-DAY MENU PLAN FOR 11–15-YEAR-OLDS

Monday

Breakfast	Porridge made with milk and water
	Raisins
Lunchbox	Bagel with low-fat soft cheese and tinned salmon or tuna
	Cherry tomatoes
	1 pot of yoghurt
	Fresh fruit
	Bottle of water
Dinner	Vegetable soup with pasta (*see* recipe page 141)
	Wholemeal roll
	Raspberry fool (*see* recipe page 214)

Tuesday

Breakfast	English muffin or bagel with jam or honey
	Yoghurt or milk
Lunchbox	Small container of pasta salad with tuna
	Satsuma or kiwi fruit
	Small bag or pot of nuts and raisins
	Fruit juice
Dinner	Fabulous fish pie (*see* recipe page 124)
	Broccoli and carrots
	Baked bananas (*see* recipe page 147)

Wednesday

Breakfast	Wholegrain cereal with milk
	Fresh fruit
	Wholemeal toast and honey
Lunchbox	Wholemeal roll with turkey and cranberry sauce
	Crudités, e.g. cucumber, pepper and carrot strips
	Cheese portion
	Piece of fresh fruit
	Bottle of water
Dinner	Pasta with sweetcorn and tuna (*see* recipe page 126)
	Brussels sprouts or broccoli
	Pancakes (*see* recipe page 145)

SEVEN-DAY MENU PLAN FOR 11–15-YEAR-OLDS (CONTINUED)	
Thursday	
Breakfast	Mango and strawberry smoothie (*see* recipe page 156)
Lunchbox	Thermos of tomato or vegetable soup
	Wholemeal roll with cheese
	Small bag of dried apricots
	Bottle of water
Dinner	Grilled chicken
	Jacket potato
	Baby sweetcorn and sugar snap peas
Friday	
Breakfast	Muesli with milk or yoghurt
	Strawberries or raspberries
Lunchbox	Wholemeal egg and mayonnaise sandwich
	Cucumber slices
	Carton of yoghurt
	Banana muffin (*see* recipe page 150)
	Bottle of water
Dinner	Mini fish cakes (*see* recipe page 128)
	Carrots and peas
	Banana bread pudding (*see* recipe page 147)
Saturday	
Breakfast	Pancakes filled with fresh fruit (*see* recipe page 145)
Lunch	Butternut squash soup (*see* recipe page 140)
	Wholemeal roll
	Fresh fruit salad with frozen yoghurt
Dinner	Pasta turkey bolognese (*see* recipe page 123)
	Broccoli and cauliflower
	Best apple crumble (*see* recipe page 146)

SEVEN-DAY MENU PLAN FOR 11–15-YEAR-OLDS (CONTINUED)	
Sunday	
Breakfast	Boiled egg and wholemeal toast
	Nectarine or a pear
Lunch	Golden chicken (*see* recipe page 124)
	Mashed potatoes and green beans
	Fresh fruit salad with frozen yoghurt or custard
Dinner	Sardines on wholemeal toast
	Baked beans and coleslaw
	Yoghurt and fruit pudding (*see* recipe page 148)

SEVEN-DAY VEGETARIAN MENU PLAN FOR 5–10-YEAR-OLDS	
Monday	
Breakfast	Muesli with milk or yoghurt
	Orange juice
Lunchbox	Spicy bean burger (*see* recipe page 131) wrapped in foil
	Small wholemeal roll
	Crudités, e.g. carrots, peppers, cucumber
	A piece of fruit
	Carton of yoghurt
	Bottle of water
Dinner	Veggie spaghetti bolognese (*see* recipe page 130)
	Fresh fruit with custard or frozen yoghurt
Tuesday	
Breakfast	Porridge made with milk, water, honey
	Raisins
Lunchbox	Wholemeal peanut butter and cucumber sandwich
	Small bag of dried apricots
	Novelty cheese portion
	Orange juice

SEVEN-DAY VEGETARIAN MENU PLAN FOR 5–10-YEAR-OLDS (CONTINUED)	
Dinner	Broccoli and cheese soup (*see* recipe page 140)
	Wholemeal roll
	Baked bananas with chocolate buttons (*see* recipe page 147)
Wednesday	
Breakfast	Banana milkshake (*see* recipe page 155)
	Wholemeal toast and Marmite
Lunchbox	Mini-bagel filled with soft cheese and banana
	Satsuma
	Carton of custard
	Orange juice
Dinner	Potato and cheese pie (*see* recipe page 138)
	Green beans and carrots
	Baked rice pudding with fresh fruit (*see* recipe page 146)
Thursday	
Breakfast	Wholegrain cereal with milk
	Orange juice
Lunchbox	Hummus dip (*see* recipe page 149)
	Breadsticks or crackers
	Crudités, e.g. carrot, pepper and cucumber strips
	Small pot of fruit purée
	Carton of fromage frais
	Bottle of water
Dinner	Spicy lentil burgers
	Jacket potato
	Baked beans and broccoli
	Fresh fruit salad
Friday	
Breakfast	Wholemeal toast and jam or marmalade
	Fresh fruit, e.g. apple or strawberries
	Milk or yoghurt

SEVEN-DAY VEGETARIAN MENU PLAN FOR 5–10-YEAR-OLDS (CONTINUED)	
Lunchbox	Mini-pitta with grated cheese and tomato
	Small pot of nuts, e.g. almonds, cashews, peanuts
	Piece of fresh fruit
	Apple muffin (*see* recipe page 150)
	Bottle of water
Dinner	Marvellous macaroni cheese with peas (*see* recipe page 132)
	Cauliflower and broccoli
	Raspberry fool (*see* recipe page 24)
Saturday	
Breakfast	Poached egg
	Tomatoes
	Wholemeal toast with Marmite
Lunch	Carrot soup (*see* recipe page 141) with grated cheese
	Wholemeal roll
	Baked apple stuffed with raisins, chopped dates, almonds and honey
Dinner	Butter bean and leeks (*see* recipe page 135)
	New potatoes and carrots
	Yoghurt
Sunday	
Breakfast	Pancakes filled with fresh fruit (*see* recipe page 145)
	Orange juice
Lunch	Nut burgers (see recipe page 131)
	Jacket potato
	Carrots and brussels sprouts or broccoli
	Banana bread pudding (*see* recipe page 147)
Dinner	Cheese on wholemeal toast
	Tomatoes and cucumber
	Yoghurt

SEVEN-DAY VEGETARIAN MENU PLAN FOR 11–15-YEAR-OLDS	
Monday	
Breakfast	English muffin or bagel with a slice of cheese
	Fresh fruit
Lunchbox	Pot of pasta salad with red kidney beans, peppers and tomatoes
	Carton of yoghurt
	Small bag of dried fruit
	Bottle of water
Dinner	Cauliflower cheese
	Jacket potato and green beans
	Baked bananas with chocolate buttons (*see* recipe page 147)
Tuesday	
Breakfast	Wholegrain cereal with milk
	Raisins or dried apricots
Lunchbox	Wholemeal roll with sliced avocado and tomato
	Cheese portion
	Piece of fresh fruit
	Carton of milkshake
Dinner	Cheese and tomato pizza (*see* recipe page 129) with any of the suggested toppings
	Jacket potato
	Coleslaw
	Fresh fruit
Wednesday	
Breakfast	Porridge made with milk and water
	Banana
Lunchbox	Thermos of vegetable soup
	Wholemeal roll
	Small bunch of seedless grapes
	Orange juice
Dinner	Pasta with chickpeas and spinach
	Fresh fruit salad with yoghurt or custard

SEVEN-DAY VEGETARIAN MENU PLAN FOR 11–15-YEAR-OLDS (CONTINUED)	
Thursday	
Breakfast	Muesli mixed with grated apple
	Milk or yoghurt
Lunchbox	Cooked vegetarian sausage, wrapped in foil
	Wholemeal Marmite sandwich
	Small pot of nuts, e.g. almonds, cashews, peanuts
	Carton of fromage frais
	Bottle of water
Dinner	Burritos filled with beans (*see* recipe page 133)
	Salad or broccoli
	Stewed pears with raisins and honey
Friday	
Breakfast	Berry smoothie (*see* recipe page 156)
	Wholemeal toast
Lunchbox	English muffin with peanut butter and cheese
	Carrot sticks
	Carton of yoghurt
	Small bag of dried fruit
	Fruit juice
Dinner	Vegetable korma (*see* recipe page 135)
	Rice
	Fresh fruit salad
Saturday	
Breakfast	Scrambled egg with mushrooms
	Wholemeal toast
Lunch	Spicy bean burger (*see* recipe page 131)
	Wholemeal bap
	Salad
	Fresh fruit
Dinner	Jacket potato filled with stir-fried vegetables or ratatouille
	Best apple crumble (or other fruit variety – *see* recipe page 146)
	Custard or yoghurt

SEVEN-DAY VEGETARIAN MENU PLAN FOR 11–15-YEAR-OLDS (CONTINUED)	
Sunday	
Breakfast	Pancakes filled with sliced bananas and honey (*see* recipe page 145)
Lunch	Mild spiced red lentils (*see* recipe page 134)
	Rice
	Carrots and broccoli
	Baked custard with cherries (*see* recipe page 148)
Dinner	Real tomato soup (*see* recipe page 139) with grated cheese
	Wholemeal roll
	Fresh fruit

home-made chicken nuggets

These home-made chicken nuggets are far healthier than the shop-bought and takeaway versions. The wheatgerm used for the coating provides essential B vitamins (thiamin and niacin), iron and zinc. They're baked rather than fried, which reduces the fat content and makes them tasty without artificial flavour-enhancers.

MAKES 4 SERVINGS

- 3 chicken breasts, boneless, skinned
- 85 g (3 oz) wheatgerm or breadcrumbs
- ½ tsp (2.5 ml) salt
- ¼ tsp (1.25 ml) garlic powder
- Freshly ground black pepper
- 90 ml (3 fl oz) water
- 1 egg white

1 *Pre-heat the oven to 200 °C/ 400 °F/ Gas mark 6.*
2 *Cut the chicken breasts into small chunks.*
3 *Combine the wheatgerm, salt, garlic powder and a little pepper. Place the mixture in a large plastic bag.*
4 *Combine the water and egg white in a bowl. Dip the chicken pieces into the egg mixture and then drop into the plastic bag. Shake until the chicken is thoroughly coated.*
5 *Place the coated chicken pieces on an oiled baking tray. Bake for 10–15 minutes or until tender and golden brown, turning once midway through cooking.*

chicken in tomato sauce

Anything in tomato sauce will be a hit with most children so this chicken dish could help you disguise extra vegetables.

MAKES 4 SERVINGS

- 4 chicken portions, on the bone
- 2 tbsp (30 ml) olive oil
- 1 onion, chopped
- 2 garlic cloves, crushed
- 1 red and 1 green pepper, chopped
- 1 tin (400 g) chopped tomatoes
- 1 tbsp (15 ml) each of fresh basil, fresh parsley and fresh chives (alternatively, use 1 tbsp/15 ml dried mixed herbs)

1 *Pre-heat the oven to 160 °C/ 325 °F/ Gas mark 3.*
2 *Sauté the chicken portions in 1 tablespoon of the olive oil until browned. Remove with a slotted spoon and put in a casserole dish.*
3 *Heat the remaining oil. Add the onion and garlic and cook for 3 minutes.*
4 *Add the peppers and cook for a further 2 minutes. Add the tinned tomatoes and herbs and simmer for 5 minutes.*
5 *Spoon sauce over the chicken and cook in the oven for about 45 minutes.*

lean meat burgers

Low in fat and a good source of iron

These home-made meat burgers are made with lean mince and cooked without extra oil. This means they're low in fat – plus as they're home-made you know exactly what's in them!

MAKES 8 SMALL OR 4 LARGE BURGERS

- 350 g (12 oz) extra lean minced meat (beef, turkey, pork)
- 60 g (2 oz) dried breadcrumbs
- 3 tbsp (45 ml) water
- 1 small onion, chopped
- 2 tbsp (30 ml) fresh sage or parsley, chopped (or 1 tbsp/ 15 ml dried herbs)
- Freshly ground black pepper

1 *Place the minced meat, breadcrumbs, water, onion, herbs and pepper in a bowl. Mix well to combine.*
2 *Divide the mixture into 4 or 8 balls and flatten into burgers. Dry fry in a hot non-stick pan for 3–4 minutes each side. Alternatively, place the burgers on a baking sheet and cook in the oven at 200 °C/ 400 °F/ Gas mark 6 for 10–15 minutes depending on the size of the burgers.*
3 *Test by inserting a skewer into the middle of a burger – there should be no trace of pink in the meat and the juices should run clear.*

pasta turkey bolognese

Good source of protein, fibre and iron

Turkey mince is used in place of the conventional beef. It's high in protein and low in fat. Bolognese sauce is a tasty way to disguise vegetables and beans.

MAKES 4 SERVINGS

- 1 tbsp (15 ml) olive oil
- 300 g (10 oz) turkey mince
- 1 large onion, chopped
- 2 sticks of celery
- 2 carrots, grated
- 1 tin (400 g) chopped tomatoes
- 1 tin (420 g) red kidney beans
- 1 teaspoon (5 ml) dried mixed herbs
- Salt and freshly ground black pepper
- 175 g (6 oz) spaghetti or other pasta shapes (adjust the quantity according to your children's appetite)

1 *Heat the olive oil in a large pan and sauté the turkey mince until it is browned. Add the onions and cook for a further 3–4 minutes.*
2 *Add the celery and carrots and cook for a further 5 minutes until just tender.*
3 *Stir in the chopped tomatoes, red kidney beans and herbs. Bring to the boil and simmer for 5 minutes. Season with salt and black pepper.*
4 *Meanwhile, cook the pasta according to the directions on the packet. Drain, then stir into the Bolognese sauce.*

golden chicken

Good source of protein and monounsaturated fats

This is one of the easiest and healthiest ways to cook chicken and proves that you don't need fast food to tempt kids to the table.

MAKES 4 SERVINGS

- 4 chicken breasts, boneless and skinless
- 60 g (2 oz) flour
- 1 tbsp (15 ml) paprika
- 2 tbsp (30 ml) olive oil
- Salt and freshly ground black pepper to taste

1 *Pre-heat the oven to 180 °C/ 350 °F/ Gas mark 4.*
2 *Place flour and paprika in a plastic bag. Add the chicken breasts and shake until the chicken is well coated.*
3 *Put the olive oil in a baking dish. Add the chicken breasts and turn carefully in the oil. Cover with foil and bake for 20 minutes.*
4 *Remove the foil and bake for a further 10 minutes until the chicken is golden brown.*

fabulous fish pie

Rich in protein, calcium and complex carbohydrates

This popular children's meal is made healthier by adding swede to the mashed potato. Alternatively, substitute parsnips or squash if you prefer.

MAKES 4 SERVINGS

- 300 g (10 oz) potatoes, peeled and cut into large chunks
- 300 g (10 oz) swede, peeled and cut into large chunks
- 550 g (1¼ lb) cod fillets
- 600ml (1 pint) skimmed milk
- 1 bay leaf
- 25 g (1 oz) butter
- 2 large leeks, thinly sliced
- 2 heaped tbsp (30 ml) plain flour
- Salt, freshly ground black pepper, 1 tsp (5 ml) Dijon mustard
- 60 g (2 oz) mature Cheddar cheese, grated

1 *Pre-heat the oven to 190 °C/ 375 °F/ Gas mark 5.*
2 *Cook the potatoes and swede in boiling water for about 15 minutes or until soft. Drain and mash with about one third of the milk.*
3 *Meanwhile, place the cod in a saucepan with the remaining milk and bay leaf. Bring to the boil and simmer for about 5 minutes.*
4 *Strain the milk into a jug. Roughly flake the fish.*
5 *Melt the butter in a pan, add the leeks and cook for 5 minutes until softened. Stir in the flour. Slowly add the milk, stirring continuously over a low heat until the sauce has thickened. Season with salt, pepper and Dijon mustard.*
6 *Combine the sauce with the fish. Place in a baking dish.*
7 *Cover evenly with the mashed potatoes and swede and scatter the cheese on top.*
8 *Bake for 20 minutes until the top is golden brown.*

mini chicken and vegetable parcels

Good source of protein, calcium and vitamin A

These little pies are made with filo pastry, which contains less fat than shortcrust pastry. You can substitute different vegetables for those suggested in the recipe.

MAKES 8 SMALL PARCELS

- 2 chicken breasts, skinless and boneless
- 2 tbsp (30 ml) olive oil
- 85 g (3 oz) button mushrooms, sliced
- 1 medium courgette, chopped
- 2 carrots, thinly sliced
- 2 tsp (10 ml) cornflour
- 200 ml (7 fl oz) milk
- 175 g (6 oz) filo pastry

1 *Cut the chicken into small pieces. Heat 1 tbsp of the oil in a pan. Add the chicken and sauté over a high heat for 3 minutes.*
2 *Add the vegetables and continue cooking over a moderate heat for 5–6 minutes until softened.*
3 *Stir in the cornflour. Slowly add the milk, stirring continuously until the sauce has thickened. Remove from the heat.*
4 *Cut the pastry into 24 squares each measuring 13 cm × 13 cm (5 in × 5 in). Lightly brush one square with olive oil, cover with another square and brush with oil. Cover with a third square.*
5 *Place a spoonful of the filling in the centre of the square. Brush the edges with a little water. Fold over one corner of the pastry to make a triangle and press to seal. Repeat with the remaining pastry squares until you have 8 parcels.*
6 *Place the parcels on a lightly oiled baking tray and brush with olive oil. Bake in the oven for 15–20 minutes until golden brown.*

toad-and-veggies-in-the-hole

Rich in protein, vitamin A and calcium

This variation of Toad-in-the-Hole includes tasty root vegetables, which add extra vitamins and fibre to the meal. It is a good dish to serve to vegetarians, too, as you can substitute vegetarian sausages for the meat ones.

MAKES 4 SERVINGS

- 4 carrots
- 1 parsnip
- 225 g (8 oz) butternut squash
- 2 tbsp (30 ml) sunflower oil
- 4 lean beef sausages or vegetarian sausages
- 125 g (4 oz) plain flour
- 1 egg
- 300 ml (½ pt) milk

1 *Pre-heat the oven to 190 °C/ 375 °F/ Gas mark 5.*
2 *Cut the vegetables into 2.5 cm (1 in) chunks. Place in a roasting tin, drizzle over the sunflower oil and toss to coat. Bake in the oven for 20 minutes.*
3 *Prick the sausages. Add to the roasting tin and cook in the oven for a further 10 minutes.*
4 *Meanwhile, make the batter. Place the flour, egg and milk in a liquidiser and blend until smooth.*
5 *Spoon the roasted vegetables and sausages into a rectangular dish. Pour over the batter and bake for a further 40 minutes until the batter has risen and is crisp on the outside.*

pasta with sweetcorn and tuna

Provides protein, complex carbohydrates and fibre

This dish is quick to prepare and makes a good midweek standby. It's also good eaten cold as a lunchbox salad.

MAKES 4 SERVINGS

- 175 g (6 oz) pasta shapes (adjust the quantity according to your children's appetite)
- 1 tbsp (15 ml) olive oil
- 1 onion, chopped
- 1 garlic clove, crushed
- 1 tin (400 g/14 oz) chopped tomatoes
- 1 tbsp (15 ml) tomato purée
- 125 g (4 oz) sweetcorn
- 1 tin (200 g/7 oz) of tuna in water or brine, drained and flaked
- 1 tsp (5 ml) dried basil

1 Cook the pasta according to the directions on the packet. Drain.
2 Meanwhile, place the onion, garlic and tomatoes in a large non-stick frying pan and cook for 4–5 minutes until onion is soft.
3 Stir in the tomato purée, chopped tomatoes and sweetcorn and cook for 5 minutes.
4 Add the tuna and basil and heat through.
5 Stir the sweetcorn and tuna sauce into the pasta and serve.

pasta with ham and mushroom sauce

Good source of complex carbohydrates, protein and calcium

MAKES 4 SERVINGS

- 175 g (6 oz) pasta shells (adjust quantity depending on appetite)
- 1 tbsp (15 ml) olive oil
- 4 slices (125 g/ 4 oz) ham (preferably reduced salt), chopped
- 125 g (4 oz) small mushrooms, halved
- 1 tbsp (15 ml) cornflour
- 300ml (½ pt) milk
- 1 tsp (5ml) dried oregano
- Freshly ground black pepper

1 Cook the pasta according to directions on the packet. Drain.
2 Meanwhile, heat the olive oil in a large frying pan. Cook the ham and mushrooms for 4–5 minutes.
3 Stir in the cornflour together with a little milk. Gradually add the rest of the milk, stirring continuously.
4 Heat until the sauce just reaches boiling point. Remove from the heat and stir in the herbs and pepper.
5 Combine with the cooked pasta.

easy chilli

Rich in iron, zinc and fibre

This version of the classic dish smuggles in extra vegetables. You may use any type of lean minced meat such as turkey, beef or pork.

MAKES 4 SERVINGS

- 225 g (8 oz) lean minced turkey, beef or pork
- 1 tbsp (15 ml) olive oil
- 1 onion, chopped
- 1 garlic clove, crushed
- 1 green pepper, chopped
- 1 celery stick, chopped
- 85 g (3 oz) button mushrooms, whole or cut in half
- 1 tsp (5 ml) paprika
- 1 pinch chilli powder (according to your children's tastes)
- ½ tsp (2.5 ml) ground cumin
- 2 tbsp (30 ml) tomato purée
- 400 ml (¾ pt) stock or water
- 1 tin (420 g/14½ oz) red kidney beans

1 Dry-fry the mince in a non-stick pan for about 5 minutes until browned. Drain off any fat. Set aside.
2 Heat the olive oil in a large pan and sauté the onion, pepper, celery, mushrooms and garlic for about 3 minutes. Add the spices and fry for a further minute.
3 Add the tomato purée, stock or water, and the beans. Cover and simmer for about 1 hour.

risotto with chicken and veggies

Packed with protein and antioxidants

Peppers are bursting with vitamin C and other antioxidants. This recipe is a delicious way of introducing them to children.

MAKES 4 SERVINGS

- 1 tbsp (15 ml) olive oil
- 1 onion, chopped
- 1 red pepper, cut into thin strips
- 1 yellow pepper, cut into thin strips
- 175 g (6 oz) long-grain or Arborio rice
- 1 litre (1½ pt) chicken or vegetable stock
- 125 g (4 oz) cooked chicken, chopped
- 25 g (1 oz) Parmesan cheese, grated
- Handful of fresh chives or parsley, if available

1 Heat the olive oil in a large saucepan.
2 Sauté the onion and peppers over a moderate heat for about 7 minutes.
3 Add the rice and cook for 2–3 minutes until the rice is translucent. Add the stock and bring to the boil, partially cover with a lid, and simmer for 12–15 minutes until the rice is tender and the liquid has been absorbed. Add a little more stock if the risotto becomes dry.
4 Add the chicken and half the Parmesan. Heat through for a few minutes.
5 Serve topped with the remaining Parmesan and herbs.

MAIN MEALS

risotto with haddock

A vitamin-rich dish

MAKES 4 SERVINGS

- 2 tbsp (30 ml) olive oil
- 1 onion, chopped
- 175 g (6 oz) long-grain or Arborio rice
- 600 ml (1 pt) vegetable stock*
- 1 bay leaf
- 350 g (12 oz) smoked haddock fillet
- 200 g (7 oz) frozen peas
- Salt and freshly ground black pepper

*Alternatively, use 2 tsp (10ml) Swiss vegetable bouillon powder or 1 vegetable stock cube dissolved in 600 ml (1 pint) water

1 *Heat the olive oil in a large saucepan. Add the rice and onion and sauté for 2–3 minutes until the rice is translucent.*
2 *Place the rice in a large pan with the stock and add the bay leaf. Bring to the boil. Cover and simmer for 15 minutes.*
3 *Add the haddock and peas and continue cooking for a further 5 minutes until the liquid has been absorbed and the fish flakes easily. Roughly break up the fish and stir the rice mixture to distribute evenly.*

mini fish cakes

Rich in omega-3 fatty acids and minerals

All fish is rich in protein and important minerals. Salmon, in particular, is rich in the essential omega-3 fatty acids, important for brain development and physical activity.

MAKES 4 LARGE OR 8 SMALL FISH CAKES

- 450 g (1 lb) potatoes, peeled
- 450 g (1 lb) salmon or cod fillet, skinned
- 60 g (2 oz) butter
- 4 tbsp (60 ml) milk
- 1 tbsp (15 ml) fresh parsley, chopped
- Salt and freshly ground black pepper

1 *Cut the potatoes into quarters and boil for 15 minutes until soft. Drain.*
2 *Meanwhile, poach the fish in water for 10 minutes. Drain and flake the fish, carefully removing all the bones.*
3 *Mash the potatoes with the butter, milk, parsley and salt and pepper. Mix in the flaked fish. Shape into 4 or 8 cakes.*
4 *Shallow fry in olive oil for a few minutes on each side. Drain on kitchen paper.*

pizzas

Making your own pizzas is easy if you have a bread machine. Alternatively, use the quick pizza base recipe as this doesn't require kneading or proving. If you haven't got time to make your own tomato sauce, use a jar of pasta sauce but remember it contains quite a lot of salt. Children will enjoy adding their own toppings, too.

Great source of complex carbohydrates, protein and calcium

MAKES 1 LARGE PIZZA OR 8 SMALL PIZZAS

Pizza base:
- 225 g (8 oz) strong white flour
- ½ sachet easy-blend yeast
- ½ tsp (2.5 ml) salt
- 175 ml (6 fl oz) warm water
- 1 tbsp (15 ml) olive oil

1 *If making the dough by hand, mix the flour, yeast and salt in a large bowl. Make a well in the centre and add the oil and half the water. Stir with a wooden spoon, gradually adding more liquid until you have a pliable dough. Turn the dough out onto a floured surface and knead for about 5 minutes until you have a smooth and elastic dough. Place the dough in a clean, lightly oiled bowl, cover with a tea towel and leave in a warm place for about 1 hour or until doubled in size.*

2 *If you are using a bread machine, place the ingredients in the tin and follow the instructions supplied with the machine.*

3 *Turn out the dough; knead briefly before rolling out on a surface to the desired shape. Alternatively, divide the dough into 8 pieces then roll each one into a circle approximately 10 cm (4 in) in diameter.*

4 *Transfer to an oiled pizza pan or baking tray and finish shaping by hand. The dough should be approx. 5 mm (¼ in) thick. For a thicker crust, let the dough rise for 30 minutes, otherwise the pizza is now ready for topping and baking.*

5 *Bake on the top shelf of the oven at 220°C/ 425°F/ Gas mark 7 for 15–20 minutes or until the topping is bubbling and the crust is golden brown.*

Quick pizza base:
- 225 g (8 oz) self-raising white flour
- 1 tsp (5 ml) baking powder
- ½ tsp (2.5 ml) salt
- 40 g (1½ oz) butter or margarine
- 150 ml (5 fl oz) skimmed milk

1 *Mix the flour, baking powder and salt in a bowl.*

2 *Rub in the butter or margarine until the mixture resembles breadcrumbs.*

3 *Add the milk, quickly mixing with a fork, just until the mixture comes together.*

4 *Roll or press the dough into a circle approx 25 cm (10 in) in diameter or shape into 8 circles approx 7 cm (3 in) in diameter and transfer onto a baking tray or pizza pan.*

5 *The base is now ready for topping. Bake on the top shelf of the oven at 220°C/ 425°F/ Gas mark 7 for 15 minutes for a large pizza or 10 minutes for smaller pizzas.*

MAIN MEALS

129

veggie spaghetti bolognese

Good source of protein, fibre and vitamins

Lentils are substituted for the meat in the Bolognese sauce. They provide plenty of protein, iron, fibre and B vitamins and make a super-tasty main course.

MAKES 4 SERVINGS

- 1 tbsp (15 ml) olive oil
- 1 onion, chopped
- 2 carrots, grated
- 1 large courgette, finely chopped
- 1 tin (400 g/14 oz) chopped tomatoes
- 1 tin (420 g/14½ oz) green lentils or 125 g (4 oz) dried lentils, soaked and cooked
- 1 tsp (5 ml) dried mixed herbs
- 175 g (6 oz) spaghetti (adjust quantity depending on appetite)
- 1 tbsp (15 ml) olive oil
- 2 tbsp (30 ml) Parmesan cheese, grated

1 *Heat the olive oil in a large frying pan. Add the vegetables, stirring often for about 5 minutes, until softened.*
2 *Add the tomatoes, lentils and herbs. Cook for a further 5–10 minutes until the sauce thickens slightly.*
3 *Meanwhile, cook the spaghetti in boiling water according to the directions on the packet. Drain and toss in a little olive oil.*
4 *Divide the spaghetti between 4 bowls. Spoon over the Bolognese sauce and sprinkle on the Parmesan cheese.*

pasta with tomato and peppers

Full of vitamin A and vitamin C

This is one of the quickest stand-by dishes in my house! You can add other vegetables, such as mushrooms, courgettes or green beans to the tomato sauce instead of peppers.

MAKES 4 SERVINGS

- 1 tbsp (15 ml) olive oil
- 1 onion, chopped
- 2 garlic cloves, crushed
- 1 red or green pepper, chopped
- 1 tin (400g/14 oz) chopped tomatoes
- 2 tbsp (30 ml) tomato purée
- 1 tsp (5 ml) dried basil
- Salt and freshly ground black pepper
- Pinch of sugar
- 175 g (6 oz) pasta shells (adjust quantity depending on appetite)
- 85 g (3 oz) Cheddar cheese, grated

1 *Heat the olive oil in a large frying pan. Add the onions, garlic and peppers and sauté for 5 minutes or until the vegetables have softened.*
2 *Add the tomatoes, tomato purée, basil, salt, pepper and sugar. Cook for 5 minutes or until the sauce thickens slightly.*
3 *Meanwhile, cook the pasta shells in boiling water according to the directions on the packet. Drain.*
4 *Combine the sauce with the pasta. Spoon into 4 dishes and sprinkle over the cheese.*

spicy bean burgers

Packed with protein and fibre

This is a favourite teatime recipe that even my children's non-vegetarian friends enjoy. The beans are a good source of protein, iron and B vitamins, but you can use other beans, such as butter beans, flageolet or cannelloni beans instead. You can also hide lots of vegetables in the burgers.

MAKES 8 SMALL OR 4 LARGE BURGERS

- 2 tins (400 g/14 oz) red kidney beans
- 1 tbsp (15 ml) olive oil
- 1 onion, chopped
- 1 clove of garlic, crushed
- 1 celery stick, chopped
- 1 carrot, finely grated
- 1 green pepper, chopped
- ½ tsp (2.5 ml) ground cumin
- ½ tsp (2.5 ml) ground coriander
- 1 tbsp (15 ml) tomato purée
- 1 tbsp (15ml) fresh coriander, chopped (optional)
- 1 egg
- 60 g (2 oz) dried breadcrumbs
- 60 g (2 oz) Cheddar cheese, grated
- Salt and freshly ground black pepper

1 Pre-heat oven to 200 °C/ 400 °F/ Gas mark 6.
2 Drain then mash the beans in a bowl.
3 Heat the oil in a frying pan and sauté the onion for 3–4 minutes until transparent. Add the garlic, celery, carrot, green pepper, spices and cook for a further 5 minutes.
4 Add the mashed beans, tomato purée, egg, breadcrumbs and cheese. Mix together then shape into 8 small or 4 large burgers.
5 Place on an oiled baking tray. Bake in the oven for 25 minutes until golden and crisp.

nut burgers

Full of healthy monounsaturated fats, minerals and vitamins

These delicious burgers are a real hit with my children. Nuts are a terrific source of essential fats, protein, iron, zinc and B vitamins. You can substitute other types of nuts, such as almonds, hazelnuts or peanuts, for the cashews if you wish.

MAKES 4 LARGE OR 8 SMALL BURGERS

- 1 onion, chopped
- 1 garlic clove, crushed
- ½ red pepper
- 1 tbsp (15 ml) rapeseed oil
- 1 tsp (5 ml) dried mixed herbs
- 1 tbsp (15 ml) wholemeal flour
- 150 ml (5 fl oz) water
- ½ vegetable stock cube
- 225 g (8 oz) cashew nuts
- 125 g (4 oz) fresh wholemeal breadcrumbs
- Salt and freshly ground black pepper
- A little olive oil for brushing

1 Pre-heat the oven to 200 °C/ 400 °F/ Gas mark 6.
2 Sauté the onion, garlic and red pepper in the oil for 5 minutes until translucent. Add the herbs and flour and continue cooking for a further 2 minutes.
3 Stir in the water and stock cube and continue stirring until the sauce has thickened.
4 Grind the cashews in a food processor then add with the breadcrumbs to the sauce. Season with salt and pepper to taste. Allow to cool slightly.
5 Shape into 4–8 burgers and arrange on an oiled baking tray. Brush lightly with a little olive oil. Bake in the oven for 15–20 minutes until golden and crisp on the outside.

marvellous macaroni cheese with peas

Packed with calcium and protein

Macaroni cheese is popular with most children. Here's a more nutritious version with peas and mushrooms, but it also works well with broad beans, carrots and red kidney beans.

MAKES 4 SERVINGS

- 175 g (6 oz) macaroni (adjust quantity depending on appetite)
- 60 g (2 oz) frozen peas
- 25 g (1 oz) butter
- 60 g (2 oz) button mushrooms, sliced
- 25 g (1 oz) cornflour
- 300 ml (½ pint) milk (full-fat or semi-skimmed)
- ½ tsp (2.5 ml) Dijon mustard
- 85 g (3 oz) mature Cheddar, grated
- Freshly ground black pepper

1 *Pre-heat the oven to 200 °C/ 400 °F/ Gas mark 6.*
2 *Cook the macaroni in boiling water according to the packet, adding the frozen peas during the last 3 minutes of cooking time. Drain.*
3 *Heat the butter in a pan. Add the mushrooms and sauté for 2 minutes.*
4 *Blend the cornflour with a little of the milk in a jug. Gradually add the remainder of the milk.*
5 *Gradually add the milk mixture to the mushrooms in the pan, stirring continuously until the sauce just reaches the boil and has thickened.*
6 *Remove from the heat, stir in mustard, half the cheese and pepper to taste.*
7 *Stir in the macaroni and peas. Spoon into an ovenproof dish, sprinkle the remaining cheese over the top and bake for 15–20 minutes until the top is bubbling and golden.*

penne with cheese and broccoli

Packed with iron and calcium

Broccoli is full of vitamin C, folate and other powerful antioxidants. This recipe is a tasty way of getting your children to eat this superfood.

MAKES 4 SERVINGS

- 175 g (6 oz) penne pasta (adjust quantity depending on appetite)
- 225 g (8 oz) broccoli florets
- 1 tbsp (15 ml) olive oil
- 1 large onion, sliced
- 1 tbsp (15 ml) cornflour
- 300 ml (½ pt) milk
- 60 g (2 oz) mature Cheddar cheese

1 *Cook the pasta in boiling water according to the directions on the packet, adding the broccoli during the last 3 minutes of cooking time. Drain.*
2 *In a non-stick pan, sauté the onion in the olive oil for 5 minutes until softened.*
3 *Blend the cornflour with a little of the milk in a jug. Gradually add the remainder of the milk. Slowly add to the onion, stirring continuously until the sauce has thickened. Stir in the cheese.*
4 *Combine with the pasta and broccoli.*

veggie lasagne

Full of protein, fibre and calcium

This dish is a firm favourite with my children. The combination of pasta, vegetables, red kidney beans and cheese makes it a near-perfect balanced meal.

MAKES 4 SERVINGS

- 1 tbsp (15 ml) olive oil
- 1 onion, chopped
- 1 red pepper, chopped
- 60 g (2 oz) mushrooms, chopped
- 1 courgette, sliced
- 1 tsp (5 ml) dried basil
- Salt and freshly ground black pepper
- 1 tin (400 g/14 oz) red kidney beans, drained
- 400 g (14 oz) passata (smooth sieved tomatoes)
- 85 g (3 oz) mature Cheddar cheese, grated
- 9 sheets lasagne (no need to pre-cook variety)

1 *Pre-heat the oven to 180°C/ 350°F/ Gas mark 4.*
2 *Heat the oil in a large frying pan. Cook the onion for 3–4 minutes. Add the other vegetables and continue cooking for 2–3 minutes.*
3 *Add the basil, salt, pepper, red kidney beans and passata. Simmer for 5 minutes until the sauce thickens slightly.*
4 *Place a layer of lasagne at the bottom of an oiled baking dish. Cover with one-third of the bean mixture. Continue with the layers, finishing with the bean mixture.*
5 *Sprinkle over the Cheddar and bake for 30 minutes until bubbling and golden.*

Burritos filled with beans

Great source of protein, fibre and iron

These tasty burritos are a new spin on pancakes, always popular with children. The bean filling is high in protein, fibre and iron.

MAKES 4 BURRITOS

- 1 tbsp (15 ml) olive oil
- 1 onion, chopped
- 1 clove of garlic, crushed
- 1 tbsp (15 ml) taco seasoning mix (according to taste)
- 1 tin (420 g/14½ oz) pinto or red kidney beans (or use 175 g/ 6 oz dried beans, soaked, cooked and drained)
- 200 g (7 oz) chopped tomatoes or 200 g (7 oz) salsa
- 4 small soft wheat tortillas
- 225 g (8 oz) passata with herbs or garlic
- 60 g (2 oz) mature Cheddar cheese, grated

1 *Pre-heat the oven to 180°C/ 350°F/ Gas mark 4.*
2 *Heat the oil in a large frying pan. Sauté the onion and garlic for 5 minutes.*
3 *Add the taco seasoning mix, kidney beans and chopped tomatoes or salsa to the pan. Roughly mash the beans and cook for a further 3 minutes until the sauce has thickened a little.*
4 *Spread one-quarter of the mixture over each tortilla. Roll up and place seam-side down in an oiled baking dish.*
5 *Spoon the passata over the tortillas; sprinkle over the cheese.*
6 *Cover with foil and bake for 20–30 minutes until golden.*

133

VEGETARIAN MEALS

chickpea and veggie hotpot

Full of protein, fibre and iron

This one-pot dish is quick and easy to prepare and makes a perfect midweek supper. Chickpeas are rich in protein, iron and zinc. Use any variety of tinned beans in place of the chickpeas, if you wish.

MAKES 4 SERVINGS

- 1 tbsp (15 ml) olive oil
- 1 onion, chopped
- 1 garlic clove, crushed
- 2 courgettes, sliced
- 1 tsp (5 ml) dried mixed herbs
- 1 tin (400g/14 oz) chopped tomatoes
- 1 tin (420 g/14½ oz) chick peas, drained
- 1 vegetable stock cube
- 40 g (1½ oz) Cheddar cheese, grated

1 *Heat the oil in a large pan and sauté the onion and garlic for 3–4 minutes until softened. Add the courgettes and cook for a further 2 minutes.*
2 *Add the herbs, tomatoes, chickpeas and crumbled stock cube. Stir well and bring to the boil. Simmer for a further 10 minutes, adding a little water if necessary.*
3 *Spoon into a baking dish, sprinkle with grated cheese.*
4 *Melt the cheese under a hot grill until the cheese is bubbling.*

mild spiced red lentils

Packed with protein, B vitamins and fibre

Red lentils are a superb source of protein, iron, fibre and B vitamins. This mildly spiced dahl will appeal to children.

MAKES 4 SERVINGS

- 1 tbsp (15 ml) sunflower oil
- 1 onion, chopped
- 1 garlic clove, crushed
- ½ tsp (2.5 ml) ground cumin
- 1 tsp (5 ml) ground coriander
- ½ tsp (2.5 ml) turmeric
- 175 g (6 oz) red lentils
- 850 ml (1½ pt) water
- Salt and freshly ground black pepper

1 *Heat the oil in a large pan and fry the onion for about 5 minutes. Add the garlic and spices and fry for a further 2 minutes.*
2 *Add the lentils and water and bring to the boil. Cover and simmer for about 30 minutes.*
3 *Season with salt and pepper to taste.*

butter bean and leeks

Rich in fibre and vitamins

This nutritious combination of pulses and vegetables is easy to prepare. You can add other vegetables, such as mushrooms or peppers, to make it a more substantial dish.

MAKES 4 SERVINGS

- 1 tbsp (15 ml) olive oil
- 2 leeks, sliced
- 1 tin (400 g/14 oz) chopped tomatoes
- 1 tin (420g/14½ oz) butter beans, drained
- 150 ml (¼ pt) vegetable stock*

*Alternatively, use ½ tsp (2.5 ml) Swiss vegetable bouillon powder or ¼ vegetable stock cube dissolved in 150 ml (¼ pt) water

1 *Sauté the leeks in the olive oil for about 5 minutes until the leeks are almost soft.*
2 *Add the remaining ingredients, stir and bring to the boil. Simmer for a further 10–15 minutes or until the sauce has thickened.*

vegetable korma

Great source of fibre, iron and zinc

Traditional kormas are made with cream. This recipe uses cashew nuts and milk in place of the cream and is a delicious way of introducing children to new flavours. Vary the vegetables according to what you have in your cupboards.

MAKES 4 SERVINGS

- 150 ml (¼ pt) milk
- 40 g (1½ oz) cashew nut pieces
- 1 tbsp (15 ml) sunflower oil
- 1 onion, sliced
- ½ tsp (2.5 ml) of each: ground cumin, garam masala and turmeric (alternatively, use 2 tsp/10 ml mild curry powder)
- 1 garlic clove, crushed
- 125 g (4 oz) cauliflower florets
- 1 courgette, sliced
- 60 g (2 oz) mushrooms
- 85 g (3 oz) baby sweetcorn
- Salt to taste

1 *Bring the milk to the boil, remove from the heat and add the cashews. Leave to soak for 15 minutes, then purée until smooth using a hand blender or food processor.*
2 *Heat the oil in a large pan and sauté the onion for 5 minutes.*
3 *Add the spices and the garlic and continue cooking for 2 minutes.*
4 *Add the vegetables, cover and simmer for 10 minutes or until the vegetables are just tender. Season with the salt.*
5 *Stir in the cashew 'cream' and simmer for a further 2 minutes.*

vegetable rice feast

Full of complex carbohydrates, vitamin C and fibre

This glorious medley of vegetables and rice is a great way of adding vegetables to children's diets. The peas and pine nuts add protein to the dish.

MAKES 4 SERVINGS

- 1 tbsp (15 ml) olive oil
- 1 onion, chopped
- 1 garlic clove, crushed
- 2 celery sticks, chopped
- 1 red or yellow pepper, chopped
- 175 g (6 oz) rice (adjust the quantity according to your children's appetite)
- 450 ml (¾ pt) vegetable stock*
- 125 g (4 oz) frozen peas
- Salt and freshly ground black pepper, to taste
- 30 g (1 oz) pine nuts
- * Alternatively, use 1½ tsp (7.5 ml) Swiss vegetable bouillon, or 1 stock cube dissolved in 450 ml (¾ pt) water

1 *Heat the oil in a large pan and sauté the onion, garlic, celery and pepper for 5 minutes.*
2 *Add the rice and stir for another 2–3 minutes.*
3 *Add the stock, bring to the boil then simmer for 15–20 minutes until the liquid has been absorbed.*
4 *Add the peas during the last 3 minutes of cooking, season to taste and heat through for a few more minutes. Serve sprinkled with the pine nuts.*

mighty root mash

Packed with complex carbohydrates, fibre and vitamins

The swede and parsnips give a subtle sweetness, which children will love. They also add extra vitamins to the dish. Extra milk is used in place of the traditional butter.

MAKES 4 SERVINGS

- 450 g (1 lb) potatoes, peeled and cubed
- 125 g (4 oz) swede, peeled and cubed
- 1 parsnip, peeled and cubed
- 200 ml (7 fl oz) milk
- Salt and freshly ground black pepper

1 *Cook the potato, swede and parsnip in a little fast-boiling water for 15–20 minutes, until tender. Drain.*
2 *Mash the root vegetables with the milk and seasoning. Add a little extra milk for a softer consistency.*

oven potato wedges

Good source of complex carbohydrates, fibre and vitamin C

These are a real treat for my children. These oven-baked wedges are healthier than chips as they are lower in fat and, with the skins left on, retain much of their vitamin C.

MAKES 4 SERVINGS

- 4 medium potatoes, scrubbed (adjust the quantity according to your children's appetite)
- 4 tsp (20 ml) sunflower or olive oil
- Optional: garlic powder; Parmesan cheese; chilli powder

1 Pre-heat the oven to 200 °C/ 400 °F/ Gas mark 6.
2 Cut each potato lengthways, then cut each half into 6 wedges.
3 Place in a baking tin and turn in the oil until each piece is lightly coated.
4 Bake for 35–40 minutes turning occasionally until the potatoes are soft inside and golden brown on the outside.
5 Sprinkle on one of the optional ingredients 5 minutes before the end of cooking.

potato tacos

Packed with complex carbohydrates, protein, iron, B vitamins and fibre

These tacos are easy to whip up and very nutritious.

MAKES 4 SERVINGS

- 4 potatoes
- ½ a 420 g (14½ oz) tin of refried beans, pinto beans or red kidney beans (roughly mashed)
- 4 tbsp (30 ml) mild taco sauce
- 125 g (4 oz) Cheddar cheese, grated
- 4 tbsp (60 ml) plain low-fat yoghurt
- Shredded iceberg lettuce
- 1 tomato, finely chopped

1 Pre-heat the oven to 200 °C/ 400 °F/ Gas mark 6.
2 Scrub the potatoes and prick with a fork. Smear with a little oil and salt – this gives a crispy jacket. Bake for about 1 hour.
3 Split the cooked potato and puff it up. Heat the mashed beans. Spoon on the beans and sauce.
4 Top with the grated cheese and yoghurt. Scatter over the lettuce and tomato.

couscous with nuts and vegetables

Packed with complex carbohydrates, fibre and healthy monounsaturated fats

Couscous is easy to prepare and children enjoy its soft texture. Mix it with vegetables and nuts and it makes a delicious balanced meal.

MAKES 4 SERVINGS

- 175 g (6 oz) couscous
- 450 ml (¾ pt) vegetable stock*
- 1 tbsp (15 ml) olive oil
- 1 onion, chopped
- 1 red pepper, chopped
- 85 g (3 oz) baby sweetcorn
- 1 carrot, diced
- 60 g (2 oz) dates, chopped (optional)
- 60 g (2 oz) flaked toasted almonds

*Alternatively, use 1½ tsp (7.5 ml) Swiss vegetable bouillon or 1 stock cube dissolved in 450 ml (¾ pt) water

1 *Bring the stock to the boil then remove from the heat. Pour over the couscous and leave to stand for 15 minutes until all the liquid has been absorbed.*
2 *Meanwhile, heat the oil in a pan and sauté the onion for 5 minutes. Add the vegetables and continue cooking for about 7–10 minutes or until the vegetables are tender-crisp (not soft).*
3 *Fluff the couscous with a fork and stir in the vegetables, almonds and dates, if using.*

potato and cheese pie

Good source of complex carbohydrates, protein and calcium

This simple dish of potatoes and cheese is a childhood favourite of mine. My children are equally fond of it. Layer sliced leeks or broccoli florets with the cheese to increase the vegetable content.

MAKES 4 SERVINGS

- 450 g (1 lb) potatoes
- 300 ml (½ pt) milk
- 60 g (2 oz) grated cheese
- 1 onion, thinly sliced
- 2 large tomatoes, sliced
- 2 eggs
- Salt and freshly ground black pepper

1 *Pre-heat the oven to 200°C/ 400°F/ Gas mark 6.*
2 *Peel and thinly slice the potatoes. Arrange layers of potato, cheese, onion and tomatoes in a shallow baking dish, finishing with cheese.*
3 *Beat the eggs with the milk, season with salt and pepper then pour over the potatoes.*
4 *Cover with foil and bake for 45–60 minutes until the potatoes are tender and the top golden brown.*

SOUPS

potato soup

Full of complex carbohydrates, vitamin A and calcium

This is an ideal main meal soup as it is rich in energy-giving carbohydrate and the milk also provides protein and calcium. Sweet potatoes provide beta-carotene and omega-3 fatty acids, essential for brain development.

MAKES 4 SERVINGS

- 2 tbsp (30 ml) olive oil
- 1 onion, chopped
- 3 medium potatoes, scrubbed and chopped into chunks
- 1 sweet potato, peeled and chopped into chunks
- 2 tsp (10 ml) Swiss vegetable bouillon powder*
- 450 ml (¾ pt) water
- 600 ml (1 pt) skimmed milk
- Freshly ground black pepper
- Handful of chopped fresh parsley or thyme, if available
- * Alternatively, use 1 vegetable stock cube

1 *Heat the oil in a large heavy-bottomed saucepan. Cook the onion on a low heat for 5 minutes until it becomes transparent.*
2 *Add the potatoes, stir and cook on a low heat for 2 minutes.*
3 *Add the vegetable bouillon powder and the water. Bring to the boil and simmer for about 20 minutes until the potatoes are soft.*
4 *Remove from the heat and mash or liquidise with the milk.*
5 *Return to the saucepan, add some freshly ground black pepper and fresh herbs. Heat through until just hot.*

real tomato soup

Bursting with vitamin C and vitamin A

Tomato soup is a firm favourite with children. It's also a great way of hiding extra vegetables, such as carrots and red peppers. This soup is packed with vitamin C, beta-carotene and the powerful antioxidant lycopene.

MAKES 4 SERVINGS

- 2 tbsp (30 ml) olive oil
- 1 onion, chopped
- 1 large carrot, grated
- 1 red pepper, chopped
- 1 large potato, peeled and cubed
- 2 garlic cloves, crushed
- 2 tsp (10 ml) Swiss vegetable bouillon powder*
- 1 tin (400 g/14 oz) chopped tomatoes
- 750 ml (1¼ pt) water
- 1 tsp (5 ml) sugar
- Freshly ground black pepper
- * Alternatively, use 1 vegetable stock cube

1 *Sauté the onion in the oil for 2–3 minutes in a large saucepan. Add the carrot, red pepper, potato and garlic and cook for a further 5 minutes.*
2 *Add the vegetable bouillon powder, tomatoes, water and sugar. Simmer for about 20 minutes or until the vegetables are soft.*
3 *Liquidise the soup using a hand blender or food processor and season with the black pepper.*

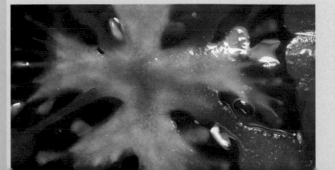

broccoli and cheese soup

Rich in iron, calcium and vitamin C

This simple soup makes a nutritionally complete meal and is an ingenious way to get children to eat broccoli. It is rich in protein, fibre, vitamin C and complex carbohydrate.

MAKES 4 SERVINGS

- 1 onion, chopped
- 300 g (10 oz) broccoli florets
- 450 ml (¾ pt) vegetable stock*
- 450 ml (¾ pt) semi-skimmed milk
- 60 g (2 oz) mature Cheddar cheese, grated
- Pinch of freshly grated nutmeg (optional)
- Salt and freshly ground black pepper

*Alternatively, use 1½ tsp (7.5 ml) Swiss vegetable bouillon powder or 1 vegetable stock cube dissolved in 450 ml (¾ pt) water

1 *Place the onion, broccoli and vegetable stock in a saucepan. Bring to the boil and simmer for about 15 minutes or until the vegetables are soft.*
2 *Liquidise the soup using a hand-held blender or food processor.*
3 *Return to the saucepan with the milk. Heat until almost at boiling point.*
4 *Add the grated Cheddar cheese, stirring until it melts.*

butternut squash soup

Bursting with beta-carotene

This is my daughter's favourite soup. Butternut squash makes a wonderful soup and its subtle sweetness appeals to children. You can substitute pumpkin or other varieties of squash for the butternut squash if you wish.

MAKES 4 SERVINGS

- 2 tbsp (30 ml) olive oil
- 1 onion, chopped
- 450 g (1 lb) butternut squash, peeled and chopped
- 1 large carrot, sliced
- 1 medium potato, peeled and chopped
- 2 tsp (10 ml) Swiss vegetable bouillon powder*
- 900 ml (1½ pts) water
- 1 tsp (5 ml) grated fresh ginger or ½ tsp (2.5 ml) ground ginger
- Freshly ground black pepper

*Alternatively, use 1 vegetable stock cube

1 *Sauté the onion in the olive oil for about 5 minutes until transparent.*
2 *Add the butternut squash, carrot and potato and cook for a further 2–3 minutes.*
3 *Add the vegetable bouillon powder and water and bring to the boil. Turn down the heat and simmer for 20 minutes or until the vegetables are tender.*
4 *Remove from the heat. Liquidise the soup using a hand-held blender or food processor.*
5 *Season with pepper.*

carrot soup

Rich in vitamin A

This soup is inexpensive and simple to make, and packed with beta-carotene which boosts immunity and helps protect the body from cancer and heart disease.

MAKES 4 SERVINGS

- 2 tbsp (30 ml) olive oil
- 1 onion, chopped
- 1 clove of garlic, crushed
- 675 g (1½ lb) carrots, sliced
- 900 ml (1½ pt) vegetable stock*
- Salt and freshly ground black pepper
- 1–2 tbsp (15–30 ml) fresh coriander, chopped (optional)

*Alternatively, use 3 tsp (15 ml) Swiss vegetable bouillon or 1½ vegetable stock cubes in 900 ml (1½ pt) water

1 *Sauté the onion and garlic in the olive oil for 5 minutes in a large saucepan.*
2 *Add the carrots and continue cooking for a further 2 minutes.*
3 *Add the stock and bring to the boil, then reduce the heat and simmer for 15 minutes or until the carrots are tender.*
4 *Season with the salt and pepper and add the fresh coriander.*
5 *Liquidise using a hand-held blender or food processor.*

vegetable soup with pasta

Full of vitamins, minerals and fibre

This soup is ideal for disguising vegetables your children may not normally choose to eat on their own. Vary the vegetables according to what you have available.

MAKES 4–6 SERVINGS

- 2 tbsp (30 ml) olive oil
- 1 onion, chopped
- 1 garlic clove, crushed
- 1 red pepper, chopped
- 1 litre (1¾ pt) vegetable stock*
- 1 tin (400 g) chopped tomatoes
- 2 large carrots, chopped
- 125 g (4 oz) cauliflower
- 2 medium potatoes, peeled and cubed
- 85 g (3 oz) small pasta shapes
- 125 g (4 oz) frozen peas
- Salt and freshly ground black pepper

*Alternatively, use 3 tsp (15 ml) Swiss bouillon or 2 vegetable stock cubes plus 1 litre (1¾ pt) water

1 *Sauté the onion, garlic and red pepper in the olive oil for 5 minutes.*
2 *Add the other vegetables except the peas and cook for a further 2 minutes. Add the vegetable stock, bring to the boil and simmer for about 20 minutes.*
3 *Add the pasta shapes and frozen peas about 10 minutes before the end of the cooking time.*
4 *Serve. Alternatively, for a chunky thick soup, liquidise half the soup after step 2 and return to the pan.*

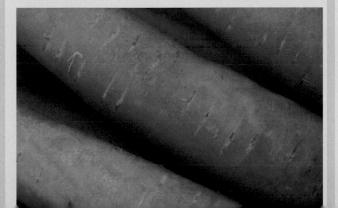

perfectly balanced salad

Rich in complex carbohydrates, protein, fibre, vitamins and minerals

This salad is an almost perfectly balanced meal. It includes foods from each food group – peppers and salad leaves from the vegetables group, raisins and apples from the fruit group, pasta from the cereal and potatoes group, nuts and yoghurt from the calcium-rich food group, red kidney beans and nuts from the protein-rich foods group, and low-fat mayonnaise from the healthy fats group.

MAKES 4 SERVINGS

- 125 g (4 oz) pasta shells
- ½ red pepper
- ½ yellow pepper
- 60 g (2 oz) toasted flaked almonds, cashews or peanuts
- 60 g (2 oz) raisins
- 125 g (4 oz) cooked or canned red kidney beans
- 2 tomatoes, sliced
- 1 apple, sliced
- Mixed salad leaves, e.g. watercress, rocket, endive or baby spinach

For the dressing:
- 3 tbsp (45 ml) low-fat mayonnaise

1 *Cook the pasta shells according to directions on the packet. Drain.*
2 *Mix the pasta with the peppers, nuts, raisins, beans, tomatoes and apple slices.*
3 *Arrange the salad leaves on a serving dish. Pile the pasta mixture on top.*
4 *Combine the low-fat mayonnaise with the salad.*

potato salad

Good source of vitamin C and complex carbohydrates

This makes an excellent portable snack or lunch. New potatoes contain twice as much vitamin C as old potatoes. You can add extra vegetables such as spring onions and radishes.

MAKES 4 SERVINGS

- 450 g (1 lb) new or old potatoes, cut into small chunks (no need to peel)
- 1 tbsp (15 ml) each of fresh chopped mint and parsley
- 15 cm (6 in) cucumber piece, diced
- 1 tbsp (15 ml) plain yoghurt
- 1 tbsp (15 ml) salad cream (or mayonnaise)
- Freshly ground black pepper

1 *Boil the potatoes in a little fast-boiling water for 5–7 minutes until just tender. Drain.*
2 *Combine the remaining ingredients together. Toss in the cooled potatoes and optional ingredients.*

bean and tuna salad

Rich in protein, B vitamins, iron and fibre

MAKES 4 SERVINGS

- 1 tin (420 g) cannelloni or butter beans, drained
- 2 tomatoes, cubed
- 1 tin (100 g) tuna in brine, drained and flaked
- 125 g (4 oz) green beans, cooked and cooled
- 1 tbsp (15 ml) red wine vinegar
- 2 tbsp (30 ml) olive oil
- Handful of fresh herbs: chives, parsley

1 *Combine the tinned beans, tomatoes, tuna and green beans in a bowl.*
2 *Mix together the vinegar, oil and herbs and combine with the salad.*

rice salad with sweetcorn

Full of complex carbohydrates, vitamin C and fibre

This salad is easy to prepare and the peppers are a great source of vitamin C. The almonds provide protein and calcium.

MAKES 4 SERVINGS

- 175 g (6 oz) rice (adjust the quantity according to your children's appetite)
- 2 red peppers, chopped
- 125 g (4 oz) sultanas
- 60 g (2 oz) split almonds, roughly chopped
- 1 tin (225 g/8 oz) sweetcorn, drained

1 *Cook the rice according to directions on the packet. Drain if necessary, rinse in cold water and drain again.*
2 *Place the cooled rice in a large bowl and combine with the remaining ingredients.*

SALADS

crunchy coleslaw

Packed with fibre and vitamins

Children love the crunchiness of shredded cabbage combined with the smooth creaminess of mayonnaise. Raw cabbage is packed with vitamin C and, though mayonnaise is high in fat, it's mostly the healthy unsaturated kind. Add any of the optional ingredients listed below to the basic recipe – it's a great way of getting your children to eat extra raw vegetables.

MAKES 4 SERVINGS

- 125 ml (4 fl oz) low-fat mayonnaise
- 1 small head of white or green cabbage, finely shredded
- 1 large carrot, peeled and grated
- Salt and freshly ground black pepper, to taste

1 *Place the cabbage and carrots in a large bowl and stir in just enough mayonnaise to moisten the vegetables. Season with salt and pepper.*
2 *Add any of the following:*
- *Chopped fresh parsley or chives*
- *Pineapple chunks*
- *Finely chopped onions or spring onions*
- *Finely chopped peppers*
- *Red cabbage*
- *Broccoli*
- *Cauliflower*
- *Raisins*
- *Cashew nuts*
- *Beetroot*
- *Sunflower seeds*
- *Toasted pumpkin seeds*
- *Grated eating apple*
- *Celery*
- *Chicory*
- *Celeriac*

salad dressings

Tasty and good for kids!

Most children reach for salad cream when confronted with raw salads. However, most shop-bought salad dressings are high in salt and contain artificial additives. Here are some quick and healthy alternatives that require no or very little preparation.

- A drizzle of balsamic vinegar
- A squeeze of lemon juice
- Plain yoghurt mixed with an equal quantity of salad cream
- Greek yoghurt mixed with a squeeze of lemon juice and chopped fresh parsley
- olive oil and vinegar dressing
- 3 tbsp (45 ml) olive oil
- 1 tbsp (15 ml) white wine vinegar or lemon juice
- Pinch of sugar
- Pinch of salt
- Freshly ground black pepper to taste

1 *Shake the ingredients together in a screw-top jar. Serving suggestion: As a dressing for leafy salads, cucumber salad and bean salads.*

pancakes

Full of protein and fibre

Pancakes are easy to make and your children will have tremendous fun tossing them! This recipe uses a half and half mixture of wholemeal and white flour to boost the vitamin, iron and fibre content. The eggs and milk are good sources of protein and the fruit fillings will provide extra vitamins.

MAKES 10–12 PANCAKES

- 70 g (2½ oz) plain white flour
- 70 g (2½ oz) plain wholemeal flour
- 2 size 3 eggs
- 250 ml (8 fl oz) milk (full-fat or semi-skimmed)
- A little vegetable oil or oil spray for frying

1 *Place all of the pancake ingredients in a liquidiser or food processor and blend until smooth.*
2 *Alternatively, mix the flours in a bowl. Make a well in the centre. Beat the egg and milk and gradually add to the flour, beating to make a smooth batter.*
3 *Place a non-stick frying pan over a high heat. Spray with oil spray or add a few drops of oil.*
4 *Pour in enough batter to coat the pan thinly and cook for 1–2 minutes until golden brown on the underside.*
5 *Turn the pancake and cook the other side for 30–60 seconds.*
6 *Turn out on a plate, cover and keep warm while you make the other pancakes.*
7 *Serve with any of the fillings below.*

Pancake fillings:
- Lemon juice and sugar
- Sliced banana mixed with a little honey
- Sliced strawberries mixed with strawberry fromage frais
- Apple purée and sultanas
- Raspberries, lightly mashed with a little sugar
- Frozen summer fruit mixture (thawed)
- Sliced mango
- Tinned pineapple
- Sliced fresh or tinned apricots mixed with a little apricot yoghurt
- Mixed berry fruits
- Tinned cherries mixed with a little Greek yoghurt
- Sliced fresh nectarines or peaches

best apple crumble

Full of vitamins, fibre and antioxidants

This is a delicious way of adding extra fruit to your children's diet. The wholemeal flour provides extra iron, fibre and B vitamins. You can make fruit crumbles with tinned fruit and frozen fruit.

MAKES 4 SERVINGS

Filling:
- 700 g (1½ lb) cooking apples, peeled and sliced
- 60 g (2 oz) raisins
- 40 g (1½ oz) sugar
- ½ tsp (2.5 ml) cinnamon
- 4 tbsp (60 ml) water

Topping:
- 60 g (2 oz) plain flour
- 60 g (2 oz) wholemeal flour
- 60 g (2 oz) butter or margarine
- 40 g (1½ oz) brown sugar

1 *Pre-heat the oven to 190 °C/ 375 °F/ Gas mark 5.*
2 *Place the apples, raisins, sugar and cinnamon in a deep baking dish. Combine well and pour the water over.*
3 *For the topping, put the flour in a bowl and rub in the butter until the mixture resembles coarse breadcrumbs. Mix in the sugar.*
4 *Sprinkle over the apples. Bake for 20–25 minutes.*

baked rice pudding

Rich in calcium and protein

This is a great-tasting nutritious pudding, simple to make and far superior to the tinned variety. Top with fresh fruit or fruit purée.

MAKES 4 SERVINGS

- 3 tbsp (45 ml) pudding rice
- 600 ml (1 pint) milk (full-fat or semi-skimmed)
- 40 g (1½ oz) sugar
- Grated nutmeg

1 *Pre-heat the oven to 150 °C/ 300 °F/ Gas mark 2.*
2 *Put the rice, milk and sugar in a 1.8 litre (3 pt) pie dish. Stir the mixture, then grate the nutmeg on top.*
3 *Bake for 1½ hours or until the milk has been absorbed and there is a light brown skin on top of the pudding.*
4 *Serve with any of the following:*
- *ready-made fruit compote*
- *stewed apples*
- *sliced peaches or nectarines*
- *stewed plums*
- *fresh raspberries, blueberries or blackberries.*

PUDDINGS

banana bread pudding

Good source of complex carbohydrates, protein and calcium

This pudding is warming and comforting, great for cold days! You can substitute raisins or stewed plums for the bananas – delicious!

MAKES 4 SERVINGS

- 6 large slices wholemeal bread
- 40 g (1½ oz) butter
- 2 small bananas, sliced
- 40 g (1½ oz) sugar
- 2 size 3 eggs
- 400 ml (14 fl oz) milk (full-fat or semi-skimmed)
- Ground cinnamon

1 *Pre-heat the oven to 180°C/ 350°F/ Gas mark 4.*
2 *Trim the crusts from the bread, spread lightly with butter and cut into quarters diagonally.*
3 *Arrange one third of the bread triangles in a lightly oiled baking dish.*
4 *Arrange one of the sliced bananas on top and repeat the layers, finishing with the bread.*
5 *Combine the sugar, eggs, and milk. Pour over the bread then sprinkle with cinnamon.*
6 *If you have time, allow to stand for 30 minutes. Bake for 40 minutes until the pudding is set and golden brown.*

baked bananas with chocolate buttons

Rich in potassium and magnesium

Easy enough for children to make themselves!

- 4 bananas
- Chocolate buttons

1 *Pre-heat the oven to 200°C/ 400°F/ Gas mark 6.*
2 *Peel the bananas. Make a slit lengthwise in each banana, not quite cutting all the way through.*
3 *Insert the chocolate buttons in the banana slits. Wrap each banana loosely in foil and place on a baking tray.*
4 *Bake in the oven for 15 minutes. Unwrap the foil parcels when cool enough and the bananas will be oozing with delicious chocolate sauce!*

chocolate-dipped fruit

Rich in vitamins and minerals

Kids will enjoy dipping the fruit in the chocolate themselves – just provide plenty of kitchen paper to wipe sticky fingers afterwards!

MAKES 4 SERVINGS

- A selection of soft fruit: strawberries, grapes, pineapple chunks, satsuma segments, pear slices
- 100 g (3.5 oz) good quality dark chocolate

1 *Break the chocolate into small pieces and melt in a bowl over a saucepan of simmering water, stirring from time to time.*
2 *Once the chocolate is melted, spear each piece of fruit with a cocktail stick and carefully dip in the chocolate, covering at least half the fruit.*
3 *Leave to set on greaseproof paper. Repeat until you have used up all the fruit (or chocolate!).*

147

yoghurt and fruit pudding

Good source of calcium and vitamins

A nutritious everyday pudding that counts towards the 5 servings of fruit or vegetables recommended for children.

MAKES 1 SERVING

- 125 g (4½ oz) carton of fruit yoghurt
- 125 g (4 oz) fresh or stewed fruit, e.g. mango, strawberries, blueberries, raspberries, peaches, bananas
- 1 tbsp (15 ml) toasted flaked almonds (or hazelnuts)

1 *Spoon half of the yoghurt into a sundae glass (or small dish).*
2 *Top with half of the fruit followed by another layer of yoghurt.*
3 *Top with the remaining fruit and nuts.*

baked custard with cherries

Rich in vitamins and calcium

This baked French custard is low in fat and a good source of protein. You can substitute other fresh or tinned fruit, such as apricots, prunes, plums or pears, for the cherries.

MAKES 4 SERVINGS

- 60 g (2 oz) plain flour
- 60 g (2 oz) sugar
- 2 size 3 eggs
- 350 ml (12 fl oz) milk
- 1 tin (400 g/14 oz) black cherries
- Pinch of grated nutmeg
- A little sunflower oil

1 *Pre-heat the oven to 200°C/ 400°F/ Gas mark 6. Lightly oil a shallow baking dish with sunflower oil.*
2 *Blend the flour, sugar, eggs and milk in a liquidiser.*
3 *Arrange the cherries evenly in the bottom of the baking dish.*
4 *Pour in the batter and sprinkle the top with nutmeg.*
5 *Bake for 40–45 minutes until the custard is firm.*

hummus

Rich in fibre, iron and protein

Hummus makes a great snack. Serve as a dip with crudités to encourage children to eat more vegetables. It also makes a satisfying sandwich filling or jacket potato topping.

MAKES ABOUT 600 ML (1 PINT)

- 225 g (8 oz) chickpeas, soaked overnight (or two 800 g/28 oz tins)
- 2 garlic cloves
- 2 tbsp (30 ml) olive oil
- 4 tbsp (60 ml) tahini
- Juice of 1 lemon
- Pinch of paprika
- Freshly ground black pepper

1 *If using dried chickpeas, drain then cook in plenty of water for about 60–90 mins or according to directions on the packet. Drain, reserving the liquid. For tinned chickpeas drain and rinse, reserving the liquid.*
2 *Purée the cooked or tinned chickpeas with the remaining ingredients with enough of the cooking liquid or juice from the tin to make a creamy consistency.*
3 *Taste and add more black pepper or lemon juice if necessary.*
4 *Chill in the fridge.*

pitta crisps

Low in fat

These pitta crisps are a healthy and tasty alternative to ordinary crisps. You can sprinkle them with a little grated cheese half way through cooking – delicious!

MAKES ABOUT 24

- 2 pitta breads (wholemeal or white)
- A little olive oil

1 *Pre-heat the oven to 200 °C/ 400 °F/ Gas mark 6.*
2 *Split the pitta breads through the middle and open out so that you have four halves.*
3 *Cut each piece into triangles. Arrange on a baking tray and bake in the oven for 5–7 minutes until they become crisp and golden.*

apple muffins

Low in fat and tasty!

These healthy muffins are excellent for lunch boxes and after-school snacks. The apples boost the nutritional value of the muffins. You can substitute apples for bananas, raisins or raspberries.

MAKES 12 MUFFINS

- 60 ml (2 fl oz) sunflower oil
- 125 g (4 oz) soft brown sugar
- 2 size 3 eggs
- 125 ml (4 fl oz) milk (full-fat or semi-skimmed)
- 1 tsp (5 ml) vanilla extract
- 2 apples, peeled, cored and grated
- 225 g (8 oz) self-raising flour

1 *Pre-heat the oven to 190 °C/ 375 °F/ Gas mark 5.*
2 *Combine the oil, sugar, eggs, milk and vanilla extract in a bowl.*
3 *Stir in the grated apples and flour.*
4 *Spoon the mixture into non-stick muffin tins. Bake for 15–20 minutes until golden brown.*

walnut and raisin bars

Rich in omega-3 fats and fibre

This recipe is a good way of adding walnuts to your children's diet. Walnuts are rich in omega-3 fats, necessary for brain development and normal eye function. You can also substitute chopped dates for the raisins.

MAKES 12

- 125 g (4 oz) wholemeal flour
- 125 g (4 oz) porridge oats
- 1 tsp (5 ml) baking powder
- 85 g (3 oz) soft brown sugar
- 1 tsp (5 ml) ground cinnamon
- 85 g (3 oz) olive oil margarine
- 1 egg
- 150 ml (5 fl oz) milk
- 85 g (3 oz) raisins
- 60 g (2 oz) chopped walnuts

1 *Pre-heat the oven to 180 °C/ 350 °F/Gas mark 4.*
2 *Lightly oil a shallow 20 cm × 20 cm baking tin.*
3 *Place the flour, oats, baking powder, sugar and cinnamon in a large bowl and mix together briefly.*
4 *Add the margarine and rub in until the mixture forms large crumbs. You may do this in an electric mixer.*
5 *Add the egg and milk and mix. The mixture should be quite runny, like porridge.*
6 *Stir in the raisins and walnuts then spoon the mixture into the prepared tin.*
7 *Bake for 20 minutes until golden brown. When cool, cut into 12 bars.*

cheese scones

Low in fat and a healthy alternative!

These cheese scones are tasty and a healthier alternative to sugary buns and cakes.

MAKES 12 SCONES

- 125 g (4 oz) self-raising wholemeal flour
- 125 g (4 oz) self-raising white flour
- 1 tsp (5 ml) baking powder
- ½ tsp (2.5 ml) mustard powder (optional)
- A pinch of salt
- 40 g (1½ oz) butter or margarine, cut into pieces
- 150 ml (¼ pint) milk (approximately)
- 60 g (2 oz) finely grated cheddar cheese
- Beaten egg or milk to glaze

1 *Preheat the oven to 210 °C/ 425 °C/ Gas mark 7.*
2 *Place the flours, salt, baking power and, if using, the mustard powder into a large bowl. Rub in the butter using your fingertips or an electric mixer until the mixture resembles fine crumbs. Stir in the cheese then mix in enough milk to give a fairly soft dough.*
3 *Turn the dough onto a floured surface and lightly press or roll out to a 2 cm thickness. Cut out about 12 scones using a small scone cutter. Place on an oiled baking sheet and brush the tops with the beaten egg or milk.*
4 *Bake for 12–15 minutes until golden and risen. Place on a wire rack to cool.*

gingerbread people

Low in fat

MAKES ABOUT 10

- 60 g (2 oz) butter or margarine
- 125 g (4 oz) soft dark brown sugar
- 4 tbsp (60 ml) golden syrup
- 225 g (8 oz) plain flour
- ½ tsp (2.5 ml) bicarbonate of soda
- 2 tsp (10 ml) ground ginger
- ½ tsp (2.5 ml) cinnamon
- 1 egg

1 *Pre-heat the oven to 190 °C/ 375 °F/ Gas mark 5. Grease a baking sheet.*
2 *Melt the butter or margarine, sugar and syrup in a saucepan.*
3 *Add the remaining ingredients and combine quickly to form a soft dough. If it is too sticky, add a little extra flour.*
4 *Roll the dough out on a floured surface then use a cutter to make the gingerbread people.*
5 *Place on the baking sheet and bake for 10 minutes or until firm to the touch and golden.*
6 *Place on a wire rack to cool. If you wish, you can decorate with icing.*

banana loaf

Good source
of fibre and
minerals

This delicious cake is made with
wholemeal flour, brown sugar and
rapeseed oil, instead of the usual white flour,
white sugar and butter.

MAKES 12 SLICES

- 225 g (8 oz) self-raising wholemeal flour
- 125 g (4 oz) brown sugar
- Pinch of salt
- ½ tsp (2.5 ml) each of mixed spice and cinnamon
- 2 large ripe bananas
- 175 ml (6 fl oz) orange juice
- 2 size 3 eggs
- 4 tbsp (60 ml) rapeseed oil

1 *Pre-heat the oven to 170 °C/ 325 °F/ Gas mark 4.*
2 *Mix together the flour, sugar, salt and spices in a bowl.*
3 *Mash the bananas with the orange juice.*
4 *Combine the mashed banana mixture, eggs and oil with the flour mixture.*
5 *Spoon into a lightly oiled 2 lb (1 kg) loaf tin.*
6 *Bake for about 1 hour. Check the cake is cooked by inserting a skewer or knife into the centre. It should come out clean.*

apple spice cake

Low in fat

This recipe is a great way of
adding extra fruit to your children's
diet. The grated apple and the rapeseed oil
make this cake deliciously moist.

MAKES 12 SLICES

- 300 g (10 oz) self-raising flour
  (half wholemeal, half white)
- 125 g (4 oz) brown sugar
- 1 tsp (5 ml) cinnamon
- 2 cooking apples, peeled and grated
- 4 tbsp (60 ml) sunflower oil
- 2 size 3 eggs
- 125 ml (4 fl oz) milk

1 *Pre-heat the oven to 170 °C/ 325 °F/ Gas mark 4.*
2 *Mix together the flour, sugar and cinnamon in a bowl.*
3 *Add the grated apple, rapeseed oil, eggs and milk and combine well.*
4 *Spoon into a lightly oiled loaf tin and bake for about 1–1¼ hours. Check the cake is done by inserting a skewer or knife into the centre. It should come out clean.*

carrot cake

Good source of fibre and vitamin A

Traditional carrot cakes have a very high oil/fat and sugar content and are smothered in cream cheese. This version is lower in fat and sugar, and is made with grated apples and carrots.

MAKES 16 SLICES

- 225 g (8 oz) self-raising flour (half wholemeal, half white)
- Pinch of salt
- 1 tsp (5ml) cinnamon
- 1 tsp (5 ml) nutmeg
- 125 g (4 oz) brown sugar
- 2 size 3 eggs
- 1 tsp (5 ml) vanilla extract
- 3 carrots, grated
- 2 apples, grated
- 4 tbsp (60 ml) rapeseed oil
- 125 ml (4 fl oz) milk

1 Pre-heat the oven to 170°C/ 325°F/ Gas mark 4.
2 Mix together the flour, salt, spices and sugar in a bowl.
3 Stir in the eggs, vanilla, carrots, apples, oil and milk.
4 Line a loaf tin or a 20 cm (8 in) round cake tin with greaseproof paper. Spoon in the cake mixture.
5 Bake for about 1 hour. Check that the cake is cooked by inserting a skewer or knife into the centre. It should come out clean.

ginger spice cake

Low in fat

This delicious cake is lower in fat and sugar than the traditional version, yet is deliciously moist as it is made with rapeseed oil.

MAKES 10 SLICES

- 200 g (7 oz) plain flour
- 1 tsp (5 ml) bicarbonate of soda
- 1 tsp (5 ml) cinnamon
- 1 tsp (5 ml) ginger
- 1 tsp (5 ml) ground cloves
- 1 size 3 egg
- 125 g (4 oz) soft brown sugar
- 4 tbsp (60 ml) sunflower oil
- 200 ml (7 oz) low-fat plain yoghurt
- 1 tbsp (15 ml) Demerara sugar
- 1 tbsp (15 ml) pecan nuts, chopped

1 Pre-heat the oven to 160°C/ 325°F/ Gas mark 3.
2 Lightly oil a 1.5 litre (2½ pint) loaf tin.
3 Place the flour, bicarbonate of soda and spices in a bowl and mix together.
4 Whisk the egg, sugar and oil together until light and fluffy. Stir in the low-fat yoghurt and mix well.
5 Gently fold in the flour and spice mixture.
6 Spoon into the prepared tin and sprinkle with the Demerara sugar and chopped nuts.
7 Bake for 45 minutes. Check the cake is cooked by inserting a skewer or knife into the centre. It should come out clean. Allow to cool for a few minutes before turning out on to a cooling rack.

wholemeal raisin biscuits

Good source of fibre

These biscuits are far healthier than bought ones. They are lower in sugar and higher in fibre.

MAKES 20 BISCUITS

- 225 g (8 oz) wholemeal plain flour
- 40 g (1½ oz) brown sugar
- 85 g (3 oz) raisins
- 2 tbsp (30 ml) rapeseed oil
- 1 size 3 egg
- 4 tbsp (60 ml) milk

1 *Pre-heat the oven to 180°C/ 350°F/ Gas mark 4.*
2 *Combine the flour, sugar and raisins in a bowl.*
3 *Stir in the oil, egg and milk and lightly mix together until you have a stiff dough.*
4 *Place spoonfuls of the mixture onto a lightly oiled baking tray.*
5 *Bake for 12–15 minutes until golden brown.*

apricot bars

Good source of vitamin A

Dried apricots are packed with beta-carotene, a powerful antioxidant that's also good for the skin.

MAKES 8 BARS

- 125 g (4 oz) self-raising white flour
- 60 g (2 oz) sugar
- 125 g (4 oz) dried apricots
- 6 tbsp (90 ml) orange juice
- 2 size 3 eggs
- 125 g (4 oz) sultanas

1 *Pre-heat the oven to 180°C/ 350°F/ Gas mark 4.*
2 *Mix together the flour and sugar in a bowl.*
3 *Blend together the apricots and juice in a liquidiser or food processor until smooth.*
4 *Add the apricot purée, eggs and sultanas to the flour and sugar. Mix together.*
5 *Spoon the mixture into an 18 cm (7 in) square cake tin. Bake for 30–35 minutes until golden brown. Allow to cool. Cut into 8 bars.*

banana shake

Good source of calcium and potassium

This simple, nutritious shake makes a great refuelling drink at any time of the day.

MAKES 2 SERVINGS

- 250 ml (8 fl oz) milk (full-fat or semi-skimmed)
- 2 ripe bananas, sliced
- Few ice cubes, crushed

1 *Put the milk, crushed ice and banana in a smoothie maker, blender or food processor. Blend until smooth, thick and bubbly.*

banana smoothie

Rich in potassium and magnesium

This velvet-thick smoothie is made simply from fruit and yoghurt, and doubles as a nourishing dessert.

MAKES 2 SERVINGS

- 1 large ripe banana
- 1 carton (150 g) plain bio-yoghurt
- 2 tsp (10 ml) honey
- 60 ml (2 fl oz) apple juice

1 *Blend all the ingredients in a smoothie maker, blender or food processor then serve.*

strawberry shake

Full of vitamin C

MAKES 2 SERVINGS

- 150 ml (¼ pt) milk (full-fat or semi-skimmed)
- 125 g (4½ oz) carton of low-fat strawberry yoghurt
- 1 handful of strawberries
- Few ice cubes, crushed

1 *Put the milk, crushed ice and strawberries in a smoothie maker, blender or food processor. Blend until smooth, thick and bubbly.*

mango and strawberry smoothie

Packed with vitamin A and C

Mangoes are a terrific source of beta-carotene, while strawberries provide lots of vitamin C. A super nutritious drink!

MAKES 2 SERVINGS

- 1 small mango
- 125 g (4 oz) strawberries
- 1 banana
- 200 ml (7 fl oz) apple juice

1 *Peel the banana and peel and stone the mango. Place all the fruit in a smoothie maker, blender or food processor and blend until smooth.*
2 *Add the apple juice and blend for a few more seconds. If you wish, you can reduce the quantity of juice to give a thicker drink.*

tropical smoothie

Bursting with vitamin C, vitamin A and fibre

The mango and papaya provide lots of beta-carotene and the lime juice is rich in vitamin C.

MAKES 2 SERVINGS

- 1 mango, peeled and stoned
- 4 slices fresh or tinned pineapple
- 1 papaya, peeled and de-seeded
- Juice of 1 lime
- Ice cubes

1 *Put the fruit and ice in a smoothie maker, blender or food processor and blend until smooth.*

peach and raspberry smoothie

Full of beta-carotene, vitamin C and potassium

This smoothie is a great energiser and immune booster.

MAKES 2 SERVINGS

- 1 banana
- 1 peach
- 125 g (4 oz) raspberries (or strawberries)
- 125 ml (4 fl oz) orange juice

1 *Place all the fruit and the orange juice in a smoothie maker, blender or food processor and blend until smooth.*

strawberry and banana shake

Great source of potassium, vitamin C and calcium

Banana and strawberries make a delicious combination. This nutritious drink makes a great after-school or post-exercise drink.

MAKES 2 SERVINGS

- 1 banana
- 125 g (4 oz) strawberries
- 1 carton (150 g) strawberry bio-yoghurt
- 120 ml (4 fl oz) milk (full-fat or semi-skimmed)

1 *Place the fruit, yoghurt and milk in a smoothie maker, blender or food processor and blend until smooth.*

berry smoothie

Rich in antioxidants

This drink is bursting with vitamin C and cancer-protective phytochemicals.

MAKES 2 SERVINGS

- 225 g (8 oz) mixture of fresh or frozen berries, e.g. raspberries, blueberries, strawberries, blackcurrants
- 150 g (5 oz) carton of raspberry bio-yoghurt
- 200 ml (7 fl oz) milk (full-fat or semi-skimmed)

1 *Put all the ingredients in a smoothie maker, blender or food processor and blend until smooth.*

further information

Sources of further information

American Dietetic Association www.eatright.org
The website of the American Dietetic Association gives nutrition news, tips and resources.

Association for the Study of Obesity www.aso.org.uk
The website of the Association for the Study of Obesity includes the Obesity Resource Information Centre (ORIC), which has information on childhood obesity.

British Dietetic Association www.bda.uk.com
The website of the British Dietetic Association includes fact sheets and information on healthy eating for children. It also provides details of registered dietitians working in private practice.

British Nutrition Foundation www.nutrition.org.uk
The website of the British Nutrition Foundation contains information, fact sheets and educational resources on nutrition and health.

Children's Food Advisory Service
www.childrensfood.org
This site set up by Organix provides information on feeding the under 5s.

The Eating Disorders Association www.edauk.com
The website of the Eating Disorders Association offers information and help on all aspects of eating disorders.

Food and Behaviour Research www.fabresearch.org
Excellent information about a wide variety of conditions where behaviour, learning and mood are linked with food and nutrition.

Food Commission www.foodcomm.org.uk
The website of the Food Commission, an independent food watchdog, contains up-to-date news of nutrition campaigns, surveys and the Parents Jury.

Food in Schools www.foodinschools.org
The Food in Schools website provides information for writing a Whole School Food Policy, as well as links to sources of further information.

Food Standards Agency www.eatwell.gov.uk
The website of the government's Food Standards Agency has news of nutrition surveys, nutrition and health information.

Grab 5! www.sustainweb.org /g5fp /index.htm
Provides top tips and practical advice on setting up a range of activities that promote healthier eating, including developing a school food policy and setting up a SNAG.

Health Education Trust www.healthedtrust.com
An excellent online resource for news and information on health for young people with useful sections on school food and drink. The site contains information about Whole School Food Policies and School Nutrition Action Groups (SNAGs).

Kids Health (The Nemours Foundation)
www.kidshealth.org
A US-based website that offers expert health, nutrition and fitness advice for parents, kids and teenagers.

Vegetarian Society www.vegsoc.org
This website provides information on vegetarian nutrition for children as well as general nutrition, health and recipes.

Weight Concern www.weightconcern.com
Excellent information on obesity issues, including a section on children's health and a BMI calculator.

Wired for Health www.wiredforhealth.gov.uk
Wired for Health is a series of websites managed on behalf of the Department of Health and the Department for Education and Skills. It provides health information that relates to the National Curriculum and the Healthy School Programme and supports a Whole School Food Policy.

general index

recipe index